Excel® **Pivot Tables & Introduction To Dashboards**
The Step-By-Step Guide

C.J. Benton

Copyright © 2017 C.J. Benton

All rights reserved.

No part of this publication may reproduced, stored in a retrieval system, or transmitted in any form or by any means, electronic, mechanical, photocopying, recording, scanning, or otherwise without signed permission from the author, except for the use of brief quotations for review purposes.

Limit Of Liability / Disclaimer Of Warranty: While the author has used their best efforts in preparing this book, they make no representations or warranties with respect to the accuracy or completeness of the contents of this book. The author does not guarantee the reader's results will match those of the author. The advice and strategies contained herein may not be suitable for your situation. The author is not engaged in offering financial, tax, legal or other professional services by publishing this book. You should consult a licensed professional where appropriate. The author shall not be liable for any errors or omissions, loss of profit or any other commercial damages including but not limited to special, incidental, consequential, or other damages.

Trademarks: Microsoft and Excel are either registered trademarks or trademarks of Microsoft Corporation in the United States and/or other countries.

ISBN-10: 1541343212
ISBN-13: 978-1541343214

Thank you!

Thank you for purchasing and reading this book! **Your feedback is valued and appreciated**. Please take a few minutes and leave a review.

Other Books Available From This Author:

1. Microsoft® Excel® **Start Here** The Beginners Guide

2. The Step-By-Step Guide To The **25 Most Common** Microsoft® Excel® Formulas & Features

3. The Step-By-Step Guide To **Pivot Tables &** Introduction To **Dashboards** *(version 2013)*

4. The Step-By-Step Guide To The **VLOOKUP** formula in Microsoft® Excel®

5. The Microsoft® Excel® Step-By-Step Training Guide **Book Bundle**

6. Excel® Macros & VBA For Business Users - A Beginners Guide

7. Microsoft® Word® Mail Merge The Step-By-Step Guide

Table of Contents

CHAPTER 1 1
- *How To Use This Book* 1

CHAPTER 2 3
- *Introduction To Pivot Tables* 3
  - What Are Pivot Tables? 3
  - What Are The Main Parts Of A Pivot Table? 5

CHAPTER 3 6
- *Building A Basic Pivot Table & Chart* 6
  - Summarizing Numbers 6
  - How To Drill-Down Pivot Table Data 11
  - Adding Additional Rows (categories) To Your Pivot Table 13
  - Charts - How To Create A Basic Pivot Table Chart...........................14

CHAPTER 4 18
- *Displaying Percentages* 18

CHAPTER 5 23
- *Ranking Results & Displaying Averages* 23
  - Displaying Averages...25
  - Ranking Data..26

CHAPTER 6 30
- *Slicers (interactive analysis) & Advanced Filtering*............................30
  - Timeline Slicer..31
  - Slicer 37
  - Advanced Filtering 41

CHAPTER 7 46
- *Introduction To Dashboards* 46
  - Adding Multiple Pivot Tables To A Worksheet 48
  - Formatting The Dashboard..60
  - Adding Charts To The Dashboard..71

CHAPTER 8 78
- *Adding Slicers and Performance Symbols To Your Dashboard* 78
  - Slicers...78
  - Performance Symbols (up/down arrows and other indicators).........82

CHAPTER 9 86
- *Refreshing Pivot Table and Dashboard Data*......................................86

CHAPTER 10	92
Protecting Your Dashboard	92
Hiding Your Pivot Table Source Data	92
Protecting The Dashboard Or Any Other Worksheet	93
CHAPTER 11	95
Grouping Pivot Table Data	95
Grouping Records	96
Count Function	99
CHAPTER 12	102
Calculated Fields In Pivot Tables	102
Adding A Basic Calculated Field	103
Changing The Display Of Formula Error Messages	113
Removing Or Changing Calculated Fields	115
Inserting Logic Fields *(if...then)*	115
CHAPTER 13	117
Creating Pivot Tables From Imported Files – using the Data Model	117
CHAPTER 14	127
Troubleshooting: Pivot Tables Displaying Duplicate Values	127
Formula - LEN	128
Formula - TRIM	131
CHAPTER 15	135
Troubleshooting: How To Resolve Common Pivot Table Errors	135
A MESSAGE FROM THE AUTHOR	138

PREFACE

For nearly twenty years, I worked as a Data & Systems Analyst for three different Fortune 500 companies, primarily in the areas of Finance, Infrastructure Services, and Logistics. During that time I used Microsoft® Excel® extensively, developing hundreds of different types of reports, analysis tools, and several forms of Dashboards.

I've utilized many Microsoft® Excel® features, including Pivot Tables. The following are the Pivot Table functions I used and taught the most to fellow colleagues.

CHAPTER 1
How To Use This Book

This book can be used as a tutorial or quick reference guide. It is intended for users who are comfortable with the basics of Microsoft® Excel® and are now ready to build upon this skill by learning Pivot Tables and Dashboards.

This book assumes you already know how to create, open, save, and modify an Excel® workbook and have a general familiarity with the Excel® toolbar (Ribbon).

All of the examples in this book use **Microsoft® Excel® 2016**, however most of the functionality and formulas can be applied with Microsoft® Excel® version 2013. All screenshots use **Microsoft® Excel® 2016,** functionality and display will be slightly different if using **Excel® 2013.**

While this book provides several basic and intermediate Pivot Table examples, the book does not cover ALL available Microsoft® Excel® Pivot Table features, formulas, and functionality.

Please always **back-up your work** and **save often**. A good best practice when attempting any new functionality is to **create a copy of the original spreadsheet** and implement your changes on the copied spreadsheet. Should anything go wrong, you then have the original spreadsheet to fall back on. Please see the diagram below.

Diagram 1:

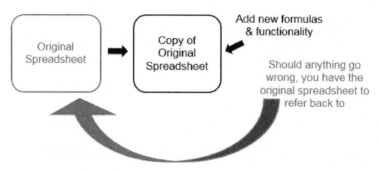

This book is structured to build on each previous chapter's teaching.

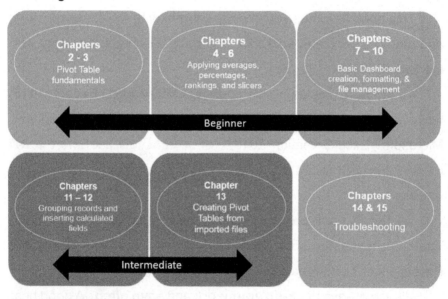

FILES FOR EXERCISES
The exercise files are available for download at the following website:
http://bentonexcelbooks.my-free.website/excel-2016

CHAPTER 2

Introduction To Pivot Tables

What Are Pivot Tables?

Pivot Tables are a feature within Microsoft® Excel® that takes individual cells or pieces of data and lets you arrange them into numerous types of calculated views. These snapshots of summarized data require minimal effort to create and can be changed by simply clicking or dragging which fields are included in your report.

By using built-in functions and filters, Pivot Tables allow you to quickly organize and summarize large amounts of data. You can filter and drill-down for more detailed examination of your numbers and various types of analysis can be completed without the need to manually enter formulas into the spreadsheet you're analyzing.

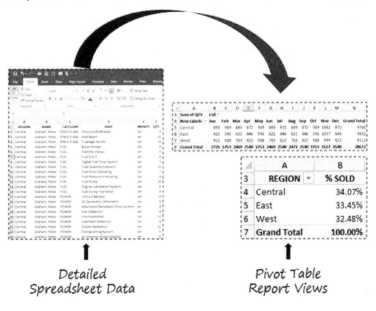

Detailed Spreadsheet Data

Pivot Table Report Views

For example, the below Pivot Table is based on a detailed spreadsheet of 3,888 individual records containing information about airplane parts. In less than 1 minute, I was able to produce the following report for the quantity of parts sold by region:

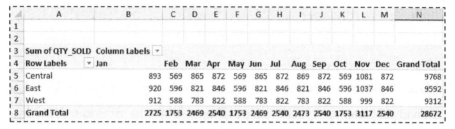

This quick summary can also be formatted to improve readability. However, formatting does require a little more time to complete.

In today's world where massive amounts of information is available, you may be tasked with analyzing significant portions of this data, perhaps consisting of several thousand or hundreds of thousands of records. You may have to reconcile numbers from many different sources and formats, such as assimilating material from:

1. Reports generated by another application, such as a legacy system
2. Data imported into Excel® via a query from a database or other application
3. Data copied or cut, and pasted into Excel® from the web or other types of screen scraping activities
4. Analyzing test or research results from multiple subjects

Excel® Pivot Tables & Introduction To Dashboards
The Step-By-Step Guide

One of the easiest ways to perform various levels analysis on this type of information and more is to use Pivot Tables.

What Are The Main Parts Of A Pivot Table?

Before we begin our first exercise, let's review the three main components of a Pivot Table:

1. **Rows:** The rows section typically represents how you would like to categorize or group your data. Some examples include: employee name, region, department, part number etc.
2. **Columns:** The columns show the level or levels in which you're displaying your calculations. Often a *time period* such as month, quarter, or year, but can also be categories, product lines, etc.
3. **Values:** Values are the calculation portion of the report, these figures can be sums, percentages, counts, averages, rankings or custom computations.

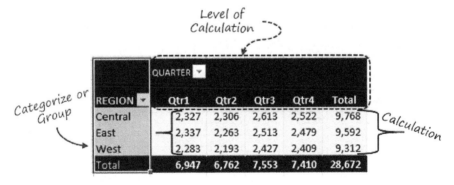

CHAPTER 3

Building A Basic Pivot Table & Chart

In this chapter we will review the fundamental steps of creating and modifying a Pivot Table. Here we will take a basic spreadsheet containing fruit sale information and:

1. Determine the total sales by region and quarter
2. Create a chart that displays the sales by region and quarter
3. Display the individual fruit sales by region and quarter

WEB ADDRESS & FILE NAME FOR EXERCISE:
http://bentonexcelbooks.my-free.website/excel-2016
FruitSales.xlsx

Summarizing Numbers

Sample data for chapters 3 - 5, due to space limitations **the entire data set is not displayed**.

	A	B	C	D	E	F	G	H	I
1	REGION	SALES PERSON FIRST NAME	SALES PERSON LAST NAME	SALES PERSON ID	QUARTER	APPLES	ORANGES	MANGOS	TOTAL
2	Central	Bob	Taylor	1174	1	1,810	2,039	1,771	5,620
3	Central	Helen	Smith	833	1	102	354	59	516
4	Central	Jill	Johnson	200	1	93	322	54	469
5	Central	Sally	Morton	500	1	595	824	556	1,975
6	Central	Sam	Becker	800	1	863	1,092	824	2,779
7	East	Abbey	Williams	690	1	346	237	260	843
8	East	John	Dower	255	1	260	178	195	633
9	East	John	Wilson	300	1	286	196	215	696
10	East	Mary	Nelson	600	1	315	215	236	766
11	East	Sarah	Taylor	900	1	381	261	285	927
12	West	Alex	Steller	1000	1	163	212	127	502
13	West	Billy	Winchester	1156	1	179	234	140	552
14	West	Helen	Simpson	817	1	148	193	116	457
15	West	Jack	Smith	100	1	111	145	87	343
16	West	Joe	Tanner	400	1	122	160	96	377
17	West	Peter	Graham	700	1	134	175	105	415
18	Central	Bob	Taylor	1174	2	113	390	65	567
19	Central	Helen	Smith	833	2	1,006	1,393	940	3,338
64	West	Joe	Tanner	400	4	2,833	2,886	2,796	8,516
65	West	Peter	Graham	700	4	4,392	4,473	4,334	13,199

Excel® Pivot Tables & Introduction To Dashboards
The Step-By-Step Guide

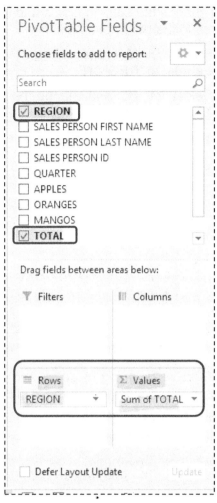

The following should be displayed on the left side of your screen
Note: the format is not very easy to read.

	A	B
1		
2		
3	Row Labels	Sum of TOTAL
4	Central	138571.3795
5	East	145587.9689
6	West	196786.7115
7	Grand Total	480946.0598

7. We can change the column labels and format of the numbers. In the below example:

   a. Select cell **'A3'** and change the text from **'Row Labels'** to **'REGION'**

   b. Select cell **'B3'** and change the text from **'Sum of TOTAL'** to **'TOTAL SALES'**

   c. You may also change the currency format in cells **'B4:B7'**. In the below example, the format was changed to U.S. dollars with zero decimal places

Below is the formatted example:

	A	B
1		
2		
3	REGION ▼	TOTAL SALES
4	Central	$ 138,571
5	East	$ 145,588
6	West	$ 196,787
7	Grand Total	$ 480,946

To enhance the report we're going to going add *Quarter columns*. This "level" dimension will provide greater detail of the total fruit sales.

8. Inside the *PivotTable Fields pane* drag the **'QUARTER'** field to the **'Columns'** section.

Note: Excel® is reading the Quarter value as numeric, therefore if you **click, instead of dragging the field** to the 'Columns' section Excel® will apply a calculation.

If this happens click the drop down-box of **'Sum of QUARTER'** in the to **'∑ Values'** section and select the option **'Move to Column Labels'**

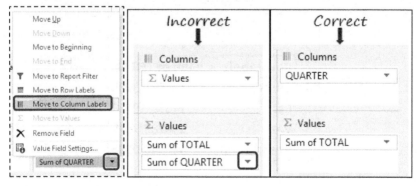

We now have **'QUARTER'** added to the summary

9. Select cell **'B3'** and change the text from **'Column Labels'** to **'BY QUARTER'**
10. The labels for cells **'B4'**, **'C4'**, **'D4'**, & **'E4'** were changed by adding the abbreviation text **'QTR'** in front of each quarter number

Before formatting:

	A	B	C	D	E	F
1						
2						
3	TOTAL SALES	Column Labels				
4	REGION	1	2	3	4	Grand Total
5	Central	$ 11,359	$ 19,352	$ 34,097	$ 73,763	$ 138,571
6	East	$ 3,865	$ 19,343	$ 38,811	$ 83,569	$ 145,588
7	West	$ 2,646	$ 23,586	$ 42,590	$ 127,964	$ 196,787
8	Grand Total	$ 17,870	$ 62,281	$ 115,499	$ 285,296	$ 480,946

After formatting:

TOTAL SALES	BY QUARTER				
REGION	QTR 1	QTR 2	QTR 3	QTR 4	Grand Total
Central	$ 11,359	$ 19,352	$ 34,097	$ 73,763	$ 138,571
East	$ 3,865	$ 19,343	$ 38,811	$ 83,569	$ 145,588
West	$ 2,646	$ 23,586	$ 42,590	$ 127,964	$ 196,787
Grand Total	$ 17,870	$ 62,281	$ 115,499	$ 285,296	$ 480,946

How To Drill-Down Pivot Table Data

Before we continue with our Pivot Table report examples, let's say you wanted to investigate further why the Central region's Q1 results are so much higher than the other two regions.

Pivot Tables allow you to **double-click on any calculated value to see the detail of that cell**. You may also **right-click** on the calculated value and select **'Show Details'**. This will create a new worksheet containing a table with the details of the calculated value.

Please see images below.

1. **Right-click** on cell **'B5'** and select **'Show Details'**

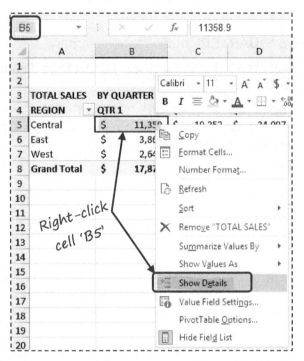

A new worksheet containing a table with the details of the calculated value in cell **'B5'**:

2. To delete the table, **right-click** on **'Sheet3'** and select **'Delete'**

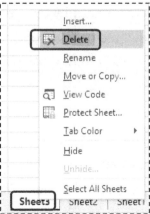

Adding Additional Rows (categories) To Your Pivot Table

From our original Pivot Table report, we'll extend our analysis by adding the individual fruit sales to our summary.

1. Drag the 'QUARTER' field from the 'COLUMNS' section to the 'ROWS' section.

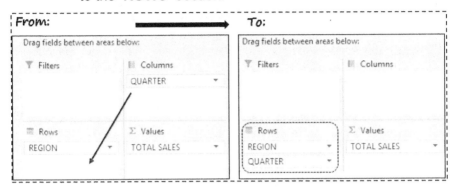

2. Drag the fields 'APPLES', 'ORANGES', & 'MANGOS' to the 'VALUES' section of the PivotTable Fields pane, place the fruit fields *before* the 'TOTAL SALES' value

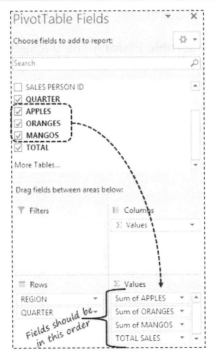

The results should look similar to the following:

REGION	Sum of APPLES	Sum of ORANGES	Sum of MANGOS	TOTAL SALES
⊟ Central	$ 43,481	$ 53,278	$ 41,812	$ 138,571
QTR 1	$ 3,463	$ 4,631	$ 3,264	$ 11,359
QTR 2	$ 5,992	$ 7,652	$ 5,709	$ 19,352
QTR 3	$ 10,634	$ 13,280	$ 10,183	$ 34,097
QTR 4	$ 23,392	$ 27,715	$ 22,656	$ 73,763
⊟ East	$ 50,626	$ 47,117	$ 47,845	$ 145,588
QTR 1	$ 1,587	$ 1,087	$ 1,190	$ 3,865
QTR 2	$ 6,891	$ 6,149	$ 6,303	$ 19,343
QTR 3	$ 13,583	$ 12,502	$ 12,726	$ 38,811
QTR 4	$ 28,564	$ 27,380	$ 27,625	$ 83,569
⊟ West	$ 69,750	$ 65,259	$ 61,778	$ 196,787
QTR 1	$ 856	$ 1,119	$ 671	$ 2,646
QTR 2	$ 7,819	$ 8,253	$ 7,513	$ 23,586
QTR 3	$ 15,335	$ 14,074	$ 13,182	$ 42,590
QTR 4	$ 45,739	$ 41,813	$ 40,411	$ 127,964
Grand Total	$ 163,857	$ 165,655	$ 151,435	$ 480,946

Charts - How To Create A Basic Pivot Table Chart

In our last example of this chapter, we'll review how to create and format a basic Pivot Table chart:

1. From the **PivotTable Fields** pane *uncheck* the '**TOTAL SALES**' field

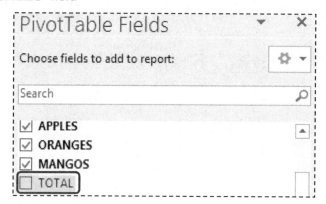

2. From the **PivotTable Tools** Ribbon select the tab **Analyze : PivotChart**

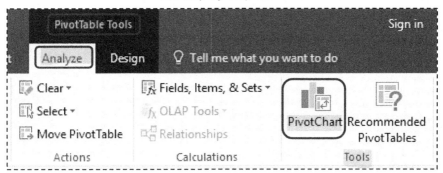

Note: *If you do not see the **PivotTable Tools** option on your Ribbon, click any PivotTable cell. This toolbar option only appears when a PivotTable field is active.*

The following dialogue box should appear:

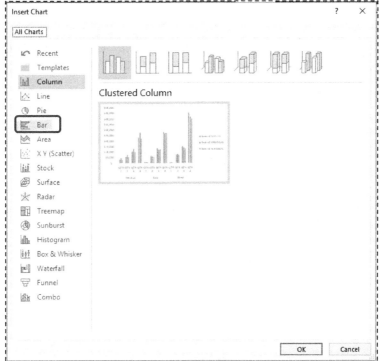

3. Select the '**Bar**' option
4. Click the '**OK**' button

A chart similar to the below should now be displayed:

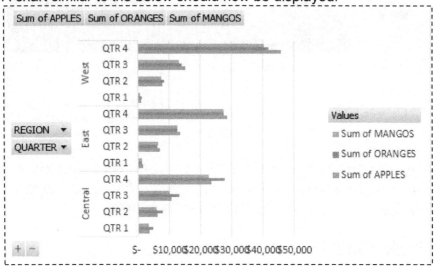

5. Drag the chart below the Pivot Table report summary and expand the width to allow for easier viewing

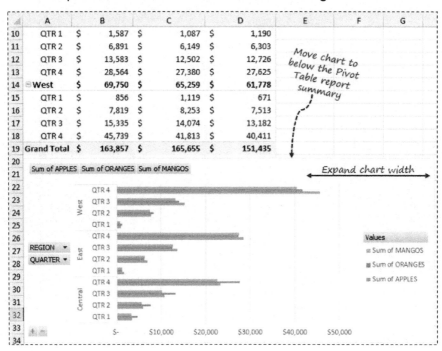

6. From the **PivotChart Tools** Ribbon select the tab **Design** and under **'Chart Styles'** select a new style

7. Edit the Chart Title by clicking inside the field, change text to **"Fruit Sales By Region & Quarter 2016"**

8. *Optional step:* hide the Field buttons, **right-click** over any Field button and select the appropriate hide option

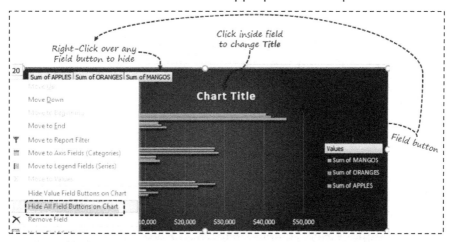

CHAPTER 4

Displaying Percentages

Another great benefit of using Pivot Tables is the ability to display numbers in various descriptive formats. In this chapter we'll describe how to use percentages to determine:

- The percentage of Individual Fruit Sales by Quarter
- The percentage of Total Sales for each Region

WEB ADDRESS & FILE NAME FOR EXERCISE:
http://bentonexcelbooks.my-free.website/excel-2016
FruitSales.xlsx

Create a new Pivot Table report, to see screenshot illustrations of steps #1 - #4, please see chapter 3 'Summarizing Numbers' page 7:

1. Open the FruitSales.xlsx spreadsheet and highlight **cells A1:I65**
2. From the Ribbon select **INSERT : PivotTable**
3. When prompted, verify the '**New Worksheet**' radio button is selected
4. Click the '**OK**' button

A new tab will be created and the *'PivotTable Fields' pane* should appear on the left side of your screen.

5. Click the following fields:
   a. Quarter *(Rows section)*
   b. Apples, Oranges, Mangos *(Values section)*

Excel® Pivot Tables & Introduction To Dashboards
The Step-By-Step Guide

A report *similar* to the following should be displayed:

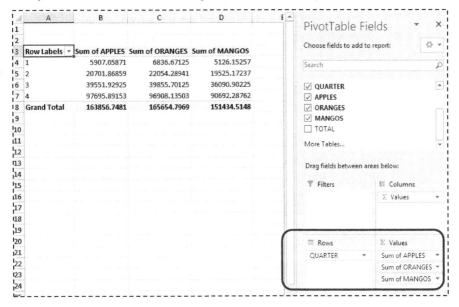

6. Click on the '**Sum of APPLES**' drop-down box and select '**Value Field Settings...**'

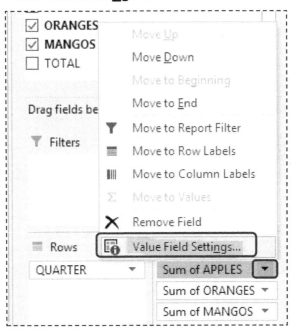

19

The following dialogue box should appear:
7. In the field '**Custom Name:**' change to **% of APPLES**
8. Select the tab '**Show Values As**'

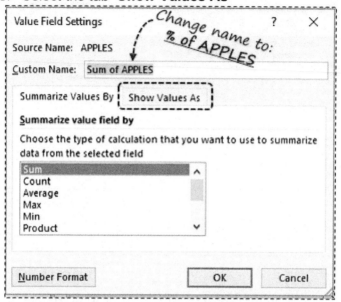

9. From the '**Show values as**' drop-down list select '**% of Grand Total**'

10. Click the '**OK**' button

Excel® Pivot Tables & Introduction To Dashboards
The Step-By-Step Guide

11. Repeat steps #6 - #10 for **'Sum of ORANGES'** and **'Sum of MANGOS'**

The totals by fruit have been changed to a percentage.

QUARTER	% of APPLES	% of ORANGES	% of MANGOS
1	3.61%	4.13%	3.39%
2	12.63%	13.31%	12.89%
3	24.14%	24.06%	23.83%
4	59.62%	58.50%	59.89%
Grand Total	100.00%	100.00%	100.00%

Please note: *In Excel®, often the percentages when summed together may exceed or not equal 100%, this is due to Excel® rounding the percentages either up or down.*

We've now answered the question, what are the percentage of Individual Fruit Sales by Quarter.

To determine the percentage of Total Sales for each Region

12. Remove (uncheck) all the fields **'APPLES,' 'ORANGES,' 'MANGOS,'** and **'QUARTER'**

13. Click the following fields:
    a. REGION (Rows section)
    b. TOTAL (Values section)

14. **Right-click** over **'Sum of TOTAL'**, (cell 'B3') from the pop-up menu select **'Show Values As'** and then **'% of Grand Total'**

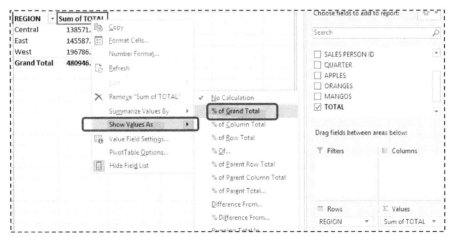

We've now determined the percentage of Total Sales for each Region.

	A	B
1		
2		
3	REGION ▼	Sum of TOTAL
4	Central	28.81%
5	East	30.27%
6	West	40.92%
7	Grand Total	100.00%

You may want to change the column heading from **'Sum of TOTAL'** to something more descriptive.

B3 ▼ : × ✓ *fx* | % OF SALES BY REGION

	A	B	C	D
1				
2				
3	REGION ▼	% OF SALES BY REGION		
4	Central	28.81%		
5	East	30.27%		
6	West	40.92%		
7	Grand Total	100.00%		

CHAPTER 5

Ranking Results & Displaying Averages

In the previous examples we focused on *summary level* types of analysis, Pivot Tables also give us the capability to analyze individual results for comparisons and ranking information. This can quickly be accomplished without the need to manually sort or add additional calculated columns to our original data source. In this chapter we'll demonstrate how to:

- Rank each Sales Person by their individual *Total & Average Sales*

WEB ADDRESS & FILE NAME FOR EXERCISE:
http://bentonexcelbooks.my-free.website/excel-2016
FruitSales.xlsx

Create a new Pivot Table report, to see screenshot illustrations of steps #1 - #4, please see chapter 3 'Summarizing Numbers' page 7:

1. Open the FruitSales.xlsx spreadsheet and highlight **cells A1:I65**
2. From the Ribbon select **INSERT : PivotTable**
3. Verify the '**New Worksheet**' radio button is selected
4. Click the '**OK**' button

A new tab will be created and the *'PivotTable Fields' pane* should appear on the left side of your screen.

5. Click the following fields:
    a. SALES PERSON ID *(Rows section)*
    b. Drag TOTAL *three* times *(Values section)*

A report *similar* to the following should be displayed. Note: all three of the '**Sum of TOTAL**' columns are currently the same. We will be changing them in the following steps.

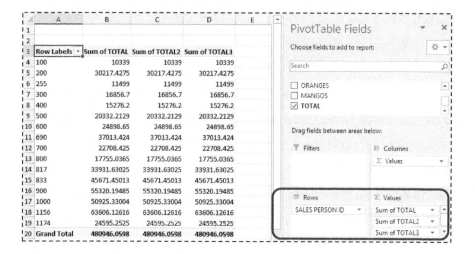

6. Change the label for cell '**A3**' to '**SALES PERSON ID**'
7. Change the label for cell '**B3**' to '**TOTAL SALES**'
8. Change the label for cell '**C3**' to '**AVERAGE SALES**'
9. Change the label for cell '**D3**' to '**RANK**'
10. Change the formatting for columns '**B**' & '**C**' to a currency of your choice with *zero decimal places*. In this example I will use the British Pound.

Please see the screenshot on the next page:

Excel® Pivot Tables & Introduction To Dashboards
The Step-By-Step Guide

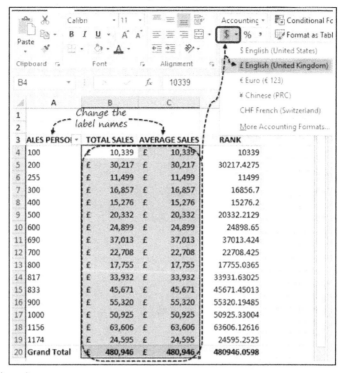

Displaying Averages

11. In the *PivotTable Fields' pane*, in the **'VALUES'** section, click the drop-down box for **'AVERAGE SALES'**

12. From the menu select the **'Value Field Settings…'** option

25

The following dialogue box should appear.

13. From the '**Summarize value field by**' list select '**Average**'. *Note: this will change the* '**Custom Name:**' *to* '**Average of TOTAL**', *change back to* '**AVERAGE SALES**'

14. Click the '**OK**' button

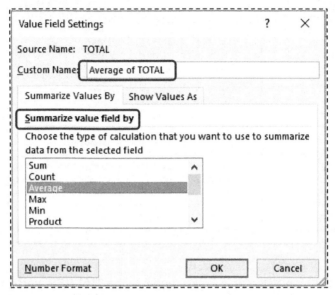

Ranking Data

15. In the *PivotTable Fields' pane*, in the '**VALUES**' section, click the drop-down box for '**RANK**'

16. From the menu select the '**Value Field Settings…**' option

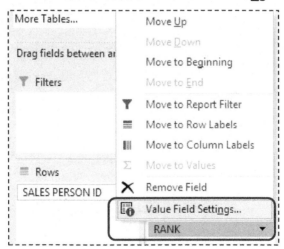

The following dialogue box should appear

17. Select the tab **'Show Values As'**
18. From the '**Show v<u>a</u>lues as**' drop-down list select **'Rank Largest to Smallest'**
19. For the **'Base field:'** box select **'SALES PERSON ID'**
20. Click the **'OK'** button

*The results should look **similar** to the following:*

	A	B	C	D
1				
2				
3	SALES PERSON	TOTAL SALES	AVERAGE SALES	RANK
4	100	£10,339	£2,585	16
5	200	£30,217	£7,554	7
6	255	£11,499	£2,875	15
7	300	£16,857	£4,214	13
8	400	£15,276	£3,819	14
9	500	£20,332	£5,083	11
10	600	£24,899	£6,225	8
11	690	£37,013	£9,253	5
12	700	£22,708	£5,677	10
13	800	£17,755	£4,439	12
14	817	£33,932	£8,483	6
15	833	£45,671	£11,418	4
16	900	£55,320	£13,830	2
17	1000	£50,925	£12,731	3
18	1156	£63,606	£15,902	1
19	1174	£24,595	£6,149	9
20	Grand Total	£480,946	£7,515	

Let's improve the readability:

> 21. With your cursor in cell '**A3**' from the **PivotTable Tools** Ribbon select the tab **Design**
> 22. Check the box '**Banded Rows**'

> 23. Place your cursor in cell '**A3**' and click the drop-down arrow
> 24. Select the option called '**More Sort Options…**'

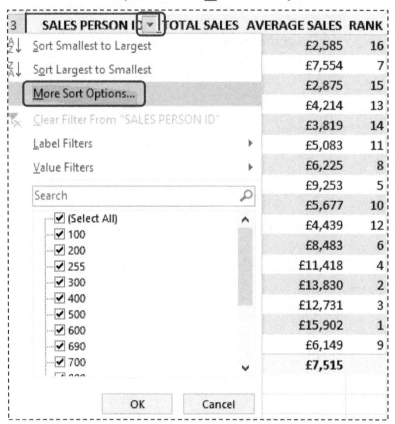

The following dialogue box will appear.

25. Select the **'Descending (Z to A) by:'** radio button
26. Select **'RANK'** from the drop-down box
27. Click the **'OK'** button

We now have a nicely formatted report that shows us each Sales Person's *sales rank* and their Total and Average Sales.

	SALES PERSON	TOTAL SALES	AVERAGE SALES	RANK
4	1156	£63,606	£15,902	1
5	900	£55,320	£13,830	2
6	1000	£50,925	£12,731	3
7	833	£45,671	£11,418	4
8	690	£37,013	£9,253	5
9	817	£33,932	£8,483	6
10	200	£30,217	£7,554	7
11	600	£24,899	£6,225	8
12	1174	£24,595	£6,149	9
13	700	£22,708	£5,677	10
14	500	£20,332	£5,083	11
15	800	£17,755	£4,439	12
16	300	£16,857	£4,214	13
17	400	£15,276	£3,819	14
18	255	£11,499	£2,875	15
19	100	£10,339	£2,585	16
20	Grand Total	£480,946	£7,515	

CHAPTER 6
Slicers (interactive analysis) & Advanced Filtering

An additional tool within the Pivot Tables feature set are 'Slicers'. Slicers are *graphical filters*, ideal for analysts or customers who like to examine data from many different perspectives. While filtering has always been a component of Pivot Tables, the introduction of the 'Timeline Slicer' has been a welcome enhancement as it allows the user to quickly categorize *individual date values* into months, quarters, or years. There are two types of slicers **1) Timeline Slicers** available in *Excel® versions 2013 & 2016* and **2) Slicers** available in *Excel® versions 2010, 2013, & 2016*.

For example, let's say you're a Financial Analyst that supports a manufacturing company of aerospace parts. You've been asked to attend an impromptu sales meeting for regional managers. The agenda *has not* been determined, instead you've been asked to prepare the sales data for the last 12 months and answer questions as they arise. Since you're unsure of what the managers will ask, you decide to create a Pivot Table report with the slicers Category & Date.

WEB ADDRESS & FILE NAME FOR EXERCISE:
http://bentonexcelbooks.my-free.website/excel-2016
AirlineParts.xlsx

EXCEL® 2013 USERS - PLEASE NOTE
Excel® 2013 users will need to follow slightly different steps for the Timeline Slicer exercise, these instructions are outlined in that specific section.

Sample data for this chapter, due to space limitations **the entire data set is not displayed**. *Note: Column 'E' is a **date value**.*

	A	B	C	D	E	F
1	REGION	NAME	CATEGORY	PART	EOM_DATE	QTY
2	Central	Graham, Peter	STRUCTURAL	Pressure Bulkheads	31 January 2017	8
3	Central	Graham, Peter	STRUCTURAL	Keel Beam	31 January 2017	11
4	Central	Graham, Peter	STRUCTURAL	Fuselage Panels	31 January 2017	13
5	Central	Graham, Peter	FUEL	Boost Pumps	31 January 2017	9
6	Central	Graham, Peter	FUEL	Transfer Valves	31 January 2017	5
7	Central	Graham, Peter	FUEL	Fuel S.O.V.	31 January 2017	6
8	Central	Graham, Peter	FUEL	Digital Fuel Flow System	31 January 2017	7
9	Central	Graham, Peter	FUEL	Fuel Quantity Indicator	31 January 2017	12
10	Central	Graham, Peter	FUEL	Fuel Flow Indicating	31 January 2017	7
11	Central	Graham, Peter	FUEL	Fuel Pressure Indicating	31 January 2017	4
12	Central	Graham, Peter	FUEL	Fuel Pump	31 January 2017	10
13	Central	Graham, Peter	FUEL	Engine Lubrication System	31 January 2017	6
14	Central	Graham, Peter	FUEL	Fuel Dump Fuel Hose	31 January 2017	9
15	Central	Graham, Peter	POWER	Lithium Battery	31 January 2017	4
16	Central	Graham, Peter	POWER	AC Generator-Alternator	31 January 2017	9
17	Central	Graham, Peter	POWER	Alternator/Generator Drive System	31 January 2017	4
18	Central	Graham, Peter	POWER	Fire Detection	31 January 2017	8
19	Central	Graham, Peter	POWER	Fire Protection	31 January 2017	13
20	Central	Graham, Peter	POWER	Overheat Detection	31 January 2017	4
21	Central	Graham, Peter	POWER	Smoke Detection	31 January 2017	11
22	Central	Graham, Peter	POWER	Extinguishing System	31 January 2017	8
23	Central	Graham, Peter	POWER	AC Inverter Phase Adapter	31 January 2017	8
24	Central	Graham, Peter	POWER	Fire Bottle-Fixed	31 January 2017	6
25	Central	Graham, Peter	POWER	AC Regulator	31 January 2017	7
3888	West	Winchester, Charles	WING	Engine Struts	31 December 2016	8
3889	West	Winchester, Charles	WING	Engine Mounts	31 December 2016	11

Timeline Slicer

Create a basic Pivot Table report, to see screenshot illustrations of steps #1 - #4, please see chapter 3 'Summarizing Numbers' page 7:

1. Open the AirlineParts.xlsx spreadsheet and highlight **cells A1:F3889**
2. From the Ribbon select **INSERT : PivotTable**
3. Verify the '**New Worksheet**' radio button is selected
4. Click the '**OK**' button

A new tab will be created and the *'PivotTable Fields' pane* should appear on the left side of your screen.

5. Click the following fields:
   a. Region *(Rows section)*
   b. Category *(Rows section)*
   c. QTY *(Values section)*

In order for a Timeline Slicer to work *all* the data for that field must be **formatted as a date**. In this example, once we click the date field,

'EOM_DATE' in Excel® 2016 will create addition calendar options **Quarters** & **Years**.

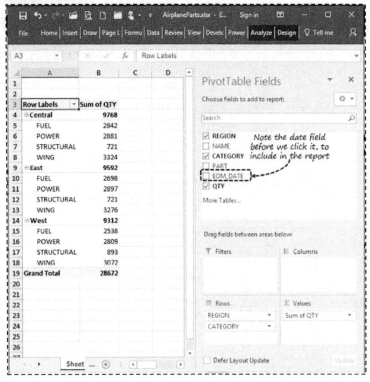

6. Click the field **'EOM_DATE'** as you can see, Excel® 2016 has created fields for **Quarters** & **Years***

*Excel 2013 users please go page 36

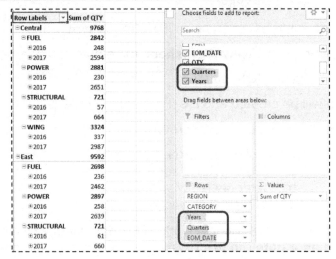

However, this type of display isn't very helpful. The Financial Analyst won't be able to quickly answer very many questions. Before adding our additional slicer, let's re-arrange the Pivot Table report to be more user friendly.

7. Uncheck fields **Years & Quarters**
8. Drag the field **'EOM_DATE'** to the **'Columns'** area. *Note: how 'EOM_DATE' is now displaying as a **month***

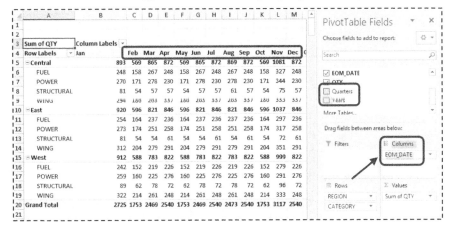

9. Insert 8 blank rows above row 3
10. With your cursor located inside the Pivot Table, from the **PivotTable Tools** Ribbon select the tab **Analyze : Insert Timeline**

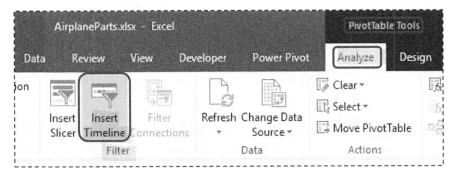

You'll receive the following prompt:

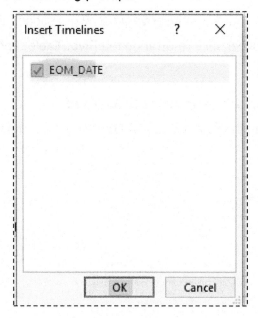

11. Click the **'EOM_DATE'** checkbox

12. Click the **'OK'** button

13. The following **Timeline slicer** should now appear, drag to the area near cell **'A1'**

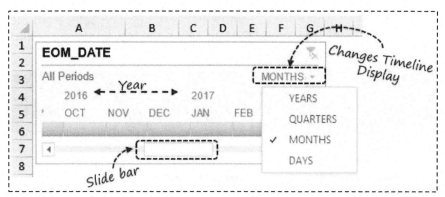

You may click individual months to view how the counts change. For example, you may click Jan 2017 or Jan and Feb 2017 to see totals change.

Excel® Pivot Tables & Introduction To Dashboards
The Step-By-Step Guide

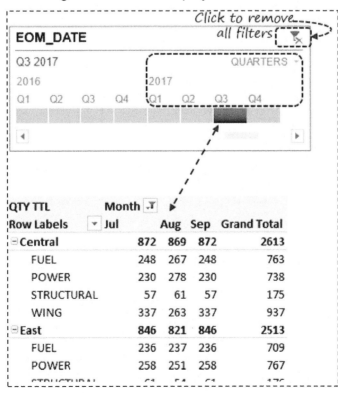

14. Change the Timeline Display from **Months** to **Quarters**

Excel 2013 users (step #6)

Users of **Excel 2013** must complete a few additional steps:

Step 6a: Select cell **'A6'**, **right-click,** and from the pop-up menu select **'Group…'**

Step 6b: When the following prompt appears, press your **'CTRL'** button on your keyboard and select **'Months'**, **'Quarters'**, & **'Years'**

Step 6c: Click the **'OK'** button

Step 6d: Return to Step #7 above

Slicer

Next, we'll review the Slicer functionality.

1. With your cursor located inside the Pivot Table, from the **PivotTable Tools** Ribbon select the tab **Analyze : Insert Slicer**

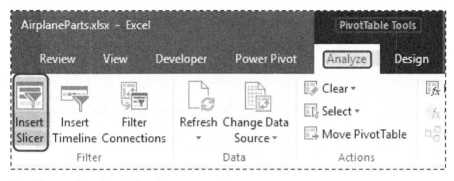

You'll receive the following prompt:

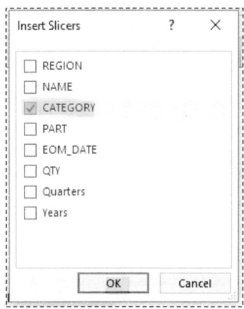

2. Click the **'CATEGORY'** checkbox
3. Click the **'OK'** button

4. The following slicer should now appear, drag to the area near cell **'H1'**

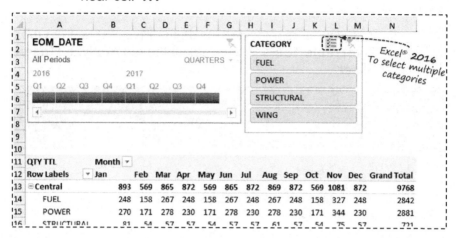

The Financial Analyst may now answer all types of questions, with just a few clicks and without having to manually re-sort or add/remove formulas. Here are some examples:

- What are the total *Fuel* sales for **Feb 2017**?
- What are the **combined** sales for the *Structural & Wing* categories only?
- Provide the **Q4** sales for *Power*

ADDITIONAL INFORMATION:

While having the date fields *Month, Quarter, & Year* automatically be added to our Pivot Table fields list is helpful, there still may be times when you want to have the **individual dates** included in your report. To see the individual date values in our current example:

1. From the *'PivotTable Fields'* pane <u>uncheck</u> fields **'REGION'** & **'CATEGORY'**
2. Drag **'EOM_DATE'** from Columns to Rows
3. From the Pivot Table **right-click** over any of the month values

4. From the pop-up menu, select **'Ungroup…'**

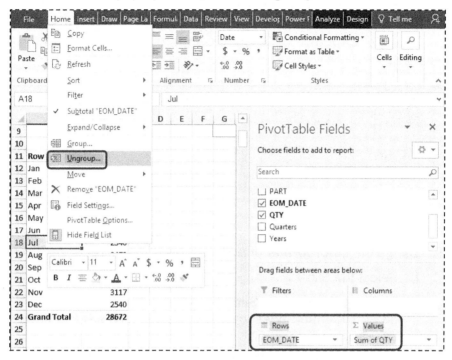

The individual dates should now be displayed:

11	Row Labels	Sum of QTY
12	31 December 2016	2540
13	31 January 2017	2725
14	28 February 2017	1753
15	31 March 2017	2469
16	30 April 2017	2540
17	31 May 2017	1753
18	30 June 2017	2469
19	31 July 2017	2540
20	31 August 2017	2473
21	30 September 2017	2540
22	31 October 2017	1753
23	30 November 2017	3117
24	Grand Total	28672

To change the *display name* of a Slicer:

1. Select the Slicer
2. From the **Timeline** or **Slicer Tools** Ribbon under **'Options'** go to **'Caption'** or **'Timeline Caption'** and enter a new name

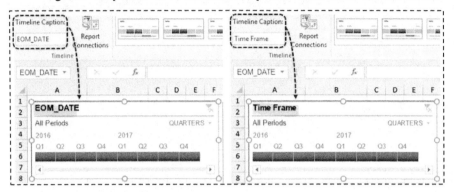

To change the *color format* of a Slicer:

1. Select the Slicer
2. From the **Timeline** or **Slicer Tools** Ribbon under **'Options'** go to **'Timeline Styles'** or **'Slicer Styles'** and select a new color scheme

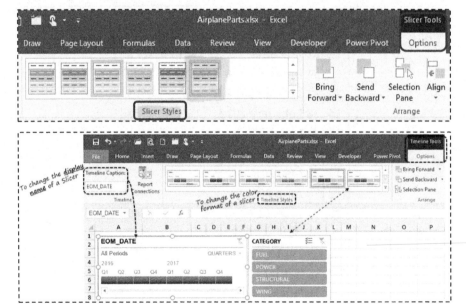

Advanced Filtering

In the first part of this chapter we reviewed how Slicers may be used for quick filtering. In this section we'll demonstrate how to employ additional Pivot Table features which allow us to extend our analysis by *specifying conditions*. For example, in the airplane parts spreadsheet, if we wanted to know:

1. The *top 10* airplane parts sold by category?
2. The *bottom 10* airplane parts sold by category?
3. The *top 10* airplane parts sold by Quarter?
4. How many parts sold more than 800 in quantity?

If you're familiar with Excel's conditional formatting capabilities, this is very similar in Pivot Tables.

Let's walk through another example to show how this functionality may be utilized.

To see screenshot illustrations of steps #1 - #4, please see chapter 3 'Summarizing Numbers' page 7:

1. Open the AirlineParts.xlsx spreadsheet and highlight **cells A1:F3889**
2. From the Ribbon select **INSERT : PivotTable**
3. Verify the '**New Worksheet**' radio button is selected
4. Click the '**OK**' button

A new tab will be created and the *'PivotTable Fields' pane* should appear on the left side of your screen.

5. Click the following fields:
   a. Part *(Rows section)*
   b. Category *(Columns section)*
   c. QTY *(Values section)*

6. Click the drop-down arrow of **'Row Labels'** cell ('A4')
7. From the menu select **'Value Filters'** then **'Top 10'**

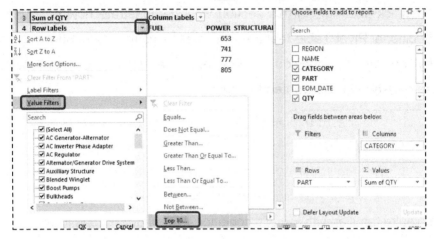

8. The following prompt will appear, click the **'OK'** button

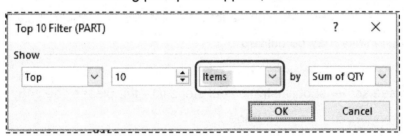

The following will be the result, you may *change the quantity from 10 to any number you would like to see*.

Sum of QTY	Column				
Row Labels	FUEL	POWER	STRUCTURAL	WING	Grand Total
Auxilliary Structure				949	949
Boost Pumps	841				841
Digital Fuel Flow System	841				841
Engine Lubrication System	849				849
Engine Struts				901	901
Fire Detection		837			837
Fire Protection		1065			1065
Fuel Dump Fuel Hose	881				881
Keel Beam			857		857
Wing Webs				849	849
Grand Total	3412	1902	857	2699	8870

Similarly we may change to show the *bottom 10*.

9. Click the drop-down arrow of **'Row Labels'**
10. From the menu select **'Value Filters'** then **'Top 10'**
11. The following prompt will appear, click the drop-down box that says **'Top'**, change to **'Bottom'**
12. Click the **'OK'** button

The following will be the result, you may *change the quantity from 10 to any number you would like to see.*

Sum of QTY	Colur				
Row Labels	FUEL	POWER	STRUCTURAL	WING	Grand Total
AC Generator-Alternator		653			653
AC Inverter Phase Adapter		741			741
Engine Mounts				705	705
Extinguishing System		709			709
Fuel Flow Indicating	741				741
Fuselage Panels			701		701
NAC/Pylon Wing Fitting				729	729
Overheat Detection		721			721
Smoke Detection		701			701
Transfer Valves	709				709
Grand Total	1450	3525	701	1434	7110

You may add a Timeline Slicer *(see page 33 for instructions)* to quickly see the *top or bottom 10 by quarter* or other time frames.

Lastly, to show how many parts sold more than 800 in quantity:

1. Click the drop-down arrow of **'Row Labels'**
2. From the menu select **'Value Filters'** then **'Greater Than…'**

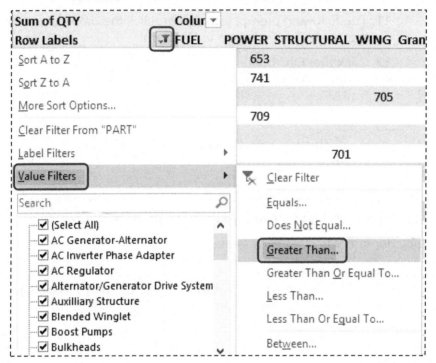

3. The following prompt will appear, enter the number **'800'** in the field after the drop-down box *'is greater than'*
4. Click the **'OK'** button

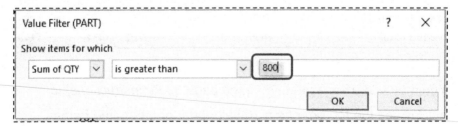

The following will be the result:

Sum of QTY Row Labels	Colur ▼ .T FUEL	POWER	STRUCTURAL	WING	Grand Total
Alternator/Generator Drive System		805			805
Auxilliary Structure				949	949
Boost Pumps	841				841
Bulkheads			801		801
Digital Fuel Flow System	841				841
Engine Lubrication System	849				849
Engine Struts				901	901
Fire Detection		837			837
Fire Protection		1065			1065
Fuel Dump Fuel Hose	881				881
Fuel Pressure Indicating	817				817
Fuel S.O.V.	821				821
Keel Beam			857		857
Lithium Battery		801			801
Longeron/Stringers				809	809
Panels				805	805
Spars				817	817
Wing Webs				849	849
Grand Total	5050	3508	857	5931	15346

To **remove a filter**:

1. Click the drop-down arrow of **'Row Labels'**
2. From the menu select **Clear Filter From "…"**

CHAPTER 7
Introduction To Dashboards

In the previous examples, we added one Pivot Table per worksheet, in this chapter we will demonstrate how to add more than one Pivot Table to a single worksheet, including how to create and format a basic Dashboard.

In chapter 9, we will illustrate how to update (Refresh) data once you have a Pivot Table or Dashboard formatted in a preferred layout.

A few things to remember when designing a new Dashboard:

A. How will your audience view the Dashboard, in paper form, on a website, mobile device? You'll want to be mindful of *spacing* and *the use of colors* if your audience reads the Dashboard on paper printed in black and white ink or limit the amount information displayed if viewing on a mobile device.

B. Does your audience require separate views of the data? Perhaps a manger is interested in only his or her own geographic area? You can add slicers to assist in filtering rather than creating separate reports for each locale.

C. What are the data sources for your Dashboard and will the data be available on the *same frequency* if you were to publish a daily or weekly basis?

D. How will you maintain your Dashboard? Will it require manual updating or will your design allow the data to be refreshed when customers open the file? *This may also depend on required permissions to access the data source.*

It's been my experience to start small when creating a Dashboard, once your customers start using the information, they almost always ask for more and request changes to the layout. You'll want to manage expectations. What seems like a simple fix to your customer may require a lot of data preparation behind the scenes. It is important to balance the amount of time you spend creating and maintaining the Dashboard with the benefits it provides.

Example:
You've been asked to create a monthly sales Dashboard to provide the following information:

1. Quantity of parts sold by region and category, including a bar graph
2. Top 10 parts sold, combined quantity and percent of total
3. A pie chart with the percent of total sales by region
4. Quantity of parts sold by region and month
   a. Include a column that shows if the total sales were *above*, *below*, or *even* with the previous month

The data is generated from a database query. You'll receive a new report at the start of every month for the prior month's sales. Users will access this report online as well as in printed form. The report <u>will not</u> be viewed on mobile devices.

The customer has included a whiteboard photo of how they would like to see the layout:

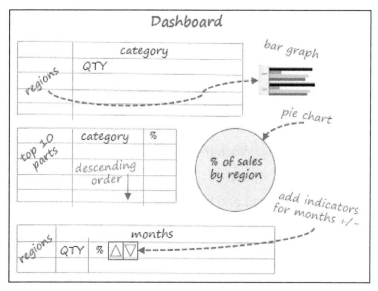

WEB ADDRESS & FILE NAME FOR EXERCISE:
http://bentonexcelbooks.my-free.website/excel-2016
DashboardData.xlsx

You've reviewed the customer's requirements and while they didn't initially ask for the ability to *filter by time period or region*, you anticipate this is something they will want and therefore decide to design accordingly. In order to build this Dashboard you will need to:

- Create 4 Pivot Tables
- Accommodate up-to 12 months of data
- Insert 2 graphs
- Add 2 slicers
- Size to fit or be *"shrunk down"* to display on one legal size (8 ½ x 14 inch) piece of paper
- Use colors on graphs and indicators sparingly, as you don't know if the paper form will be printed in color or in black and white ink

Adding Multiple Pivot Tables To A Worksheet

Pivot Table #1
Quantity of parts sold by region and category

Create a new Pivot Table report, to see screenshot illustrations of steps #1 - #4, please see chapter 3 'Summarizing Numbers' page 7:

1. Open the DashboardData.xlsx spreadsheet and highlight **columns A:F** *(select columns, not cells)*
2. From the Ribbon select **INSERT : PivotTable**
3. Select the '**New Worksheet**' radio button
4. Click the '**OK**' button

A new tab will be created and the *'PivotTable Fields' pane* should appear on the left side of your screen.

5. Rename the tab from **'Sheet1'** to **'Dashboard'**

Excel® Pivot Tables & Introduction To Dashboards
The Step-By-Step Guide

From:

To:

6. In the *'PivotTable Fields' pane* select the following fields:
   a. REGION *(Rows section)*
   b. CATEGORY *(Columns section)*
   c. QTY *(Values section)* **Please note: when adding the QTY fields, it will default to 'Count of QTY', change to 'Sum'**

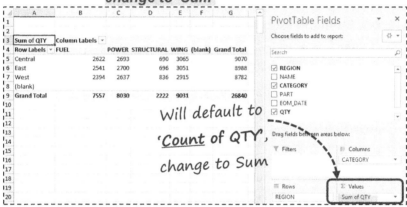

7. Change the label names:
   a. Change cell **'A3'** to QUANTITY
   b. Change cell **'A4'** to REGIONS
   c. Change cell **'B3'** to CATEGORY
   d. Change cell **'A9'** to TOTAL *(this will also change cell 'G9')*

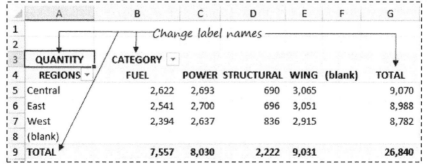

8. Change the number format for the **'QTY'** to include a comma (zero decimal places)

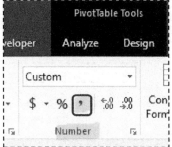

We'll add the bar chart in the last part of this chapter, page 75.

Pivot Table #2
Top 10 parts sold, combined quantity and percent of total

1. Return to the **'Data'** tab and highlight *columns* A:F
2. From the Ribbon select **INSERT : PivotTable**
3. When you receive the **Create PivotTable** prompt, select the **'Existing Worksheet'** radio button
4. Place your cursor inside the **'Location:'** box

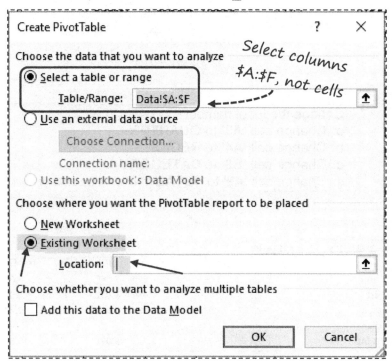

5. With your cursor still inside the **'Location:'** box click the **'Dashboard'** tab and then cell **'A11'**

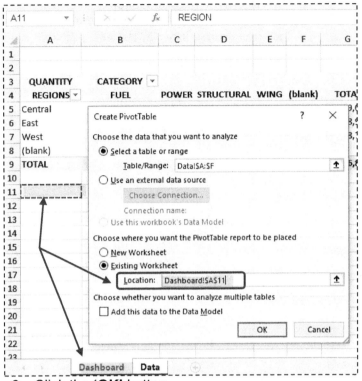

6. Click the **'OK'** button

Your screen should look similar to the following:

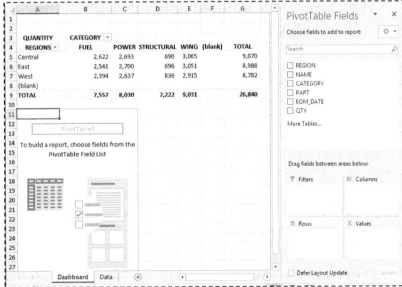

7. In the *'PivotTable Fields' pane* select the following fields:
   a. PART *(Rows section)*
   b. CATEGORY *(Rows section)*
   c. QTY *two* times *(Values section)* **Please note: when adding the QTY fields, it will default to 'Count of QTY', change to 'Sum'**

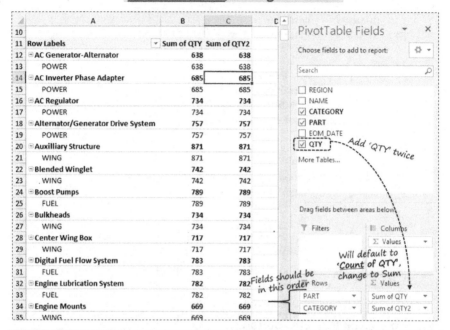

Why are the '∑ Values' fields defaulting to *Count* instead of *Sum*?

When Pivot Table source data contains blank rows, in this case because we're selecting columns (Data!$A:$F) instead of a specific cell rage (Data!$A$1:$F$3889) our source data contains *blank rows*. For some reason when this occurs Microsoft® has decided to default fields going into the '∑ Values' section to count. In order to prepare our Dashboard to receive new data, the best practice is to use columns instead of a specific cell range.

If you search the web, users have applied work arounds such as changing the blank rows to contain values of zero. For data quality and troubleshooting purposes, I do not modify source data unless required for ETL (Extract Transform Load) processes.

8. Click the drop-down arrow of **'Row Labels' (cell 'A11')**

9. From the menu select **'Value Filters'** then **'Top 10'**

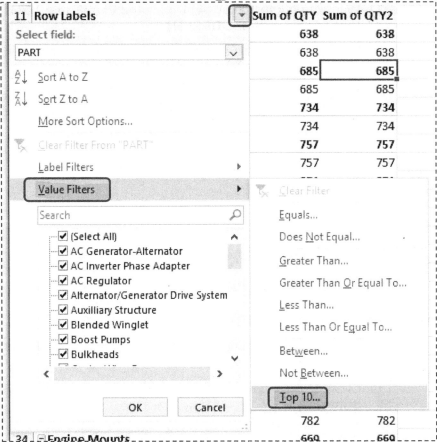

10. The following prompt will appear, click the **'OK'** button

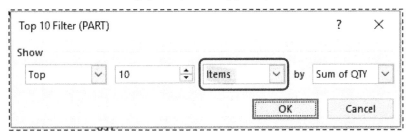

Next, we'll change the display so the **'Category'** field appears as a column

> 11. With your cursor in cell **'A11'** from the **PivotTable Tools** Ribbon select the tab **DESIGN**
>
> 12. Click the drop-down box **'Report Layout'** then **'Show in Tabular Form'**

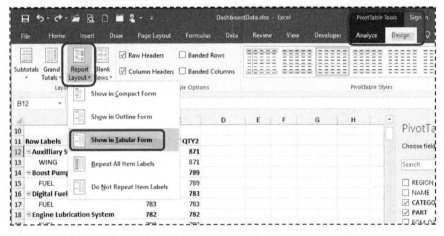

We also need to hide the 'PART' **subtotals**

> 13. With your cursor in cell **'A11'** from the **PivotTable Tools** Ribbon select the tab **DESIGN**
>
> 14. Click the drop-down box **'Subtotals'** then **'Do Not Show Subtotals**

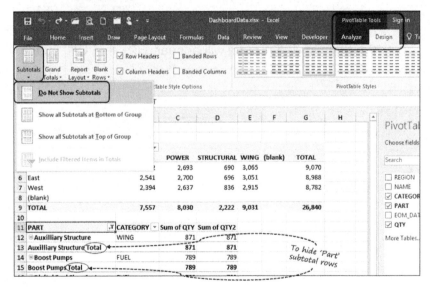

15. Click the second **'Sum of QTY'** drop-down box and select **'Value Field Settings...'**

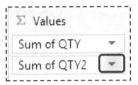

The following dialogue box should appear:

16. In the field **'Custom Name:'** change to **%**

17. From the **'Show values as'** drop-down list select **'% of Grand Total'**

18. Click the **'OK'** button

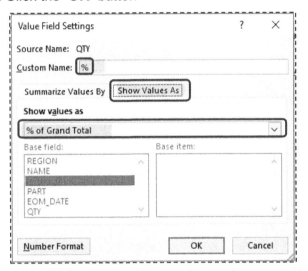

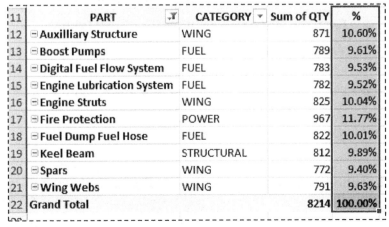

	PART	CATEGORY	Sum of QTY	%
11				
12	Auxilliary Structure	WING	871	10.60%
13	Boost Pumps	FUEL	789	9.61%
14	Digital Fuel Flow System	FUEL	783	9.53%
15	Engine Lubrication System	FUEL	782	9.52%
16	Engine Struts	WING	825	10.04%
17	Fire Protection	POWER	967	11.77%
18	Fuel Dump Fuel Hose	FUEL	822	10.01%
19	Keel Beam	STRUCTURAL	812	9.89%
20	Spars	WING	772	9.40%
21	Wing Webs	WING	791	9.63%
22	Grand Total		8214	100.00%

19. Change the label names:
    a. Change cell **'A11'** to **TOP 10 PARTS SOLD**
    b. Change cell **'C11'** to **QTY SOLD**
    c. Change cell **'A22'** to **TOTAL**

	A	B	C	D
10				
11	TOP 10 PARTS SOLD	CATEGORY	QTY SOLD	%
12	Auxilliary Structure	WING	871	10.6%
13	Boost Pumps	FUEL	789	9.6%
14	Digital Fuel Flow System	FUEL	783	9.5%
15	Engine Lubrication System	FUEL	782	9.5%
16	Engine Struts	WING	825	10.0%
17	Fire Protection	POWER	967	11.8%
18	Fuel Dump Fuel Hose	FUEL	822	10.0%
19	Keel Beam	STRUCTURAL	812	9.9%
20	Spars	WING	772	9.4%
21	Wing Webs	WING	791	9.6%
22	TOTAL		8,214	100.0%

Change label names

20. Change the number format for the **'QTY SOLD'** to include a comma (zero decimal places)

Pivot Table #3
Quantity of parts sold by region and month

1. Return to the **'Data'** tab and highlight *columns* A:F
2. From the Ribbon select **INSERT : PivotTable**
3. When you receive the **Create PivotTable** prompt, select the **'Existing Worksheet'** radio button
4. Place your cursor inside the **'Location:'** box
5. With your cursor still inside the **'Location:'** box click the **'Dashboard'** tab and then cell **'A26'**

The **'Location:'** box should now have **Dashboard!$A$26** entered

Excel® Pivot Tables & Introduction To Dashboards
The Step-By-Step Guide

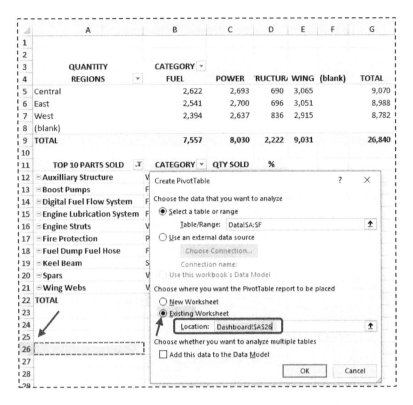

In the *'PivotTable Fields' pane* select the following fields:
   a. REGION *(Rows section)*
   b. EOM_DATE *(Columns section)*
   c. QTY *two* times *(Values section)* **Please note: when adding the QTY fields, it will default to 'Count of QTY'**

6. Click the **'Count of QTY'** drop-down box and select **'Value Field Settings...'**

57

7. In the box '**Summarize value field by**' select '**Sum**'
8. In the field '**Custom Name:**' change to **TTL**
9. Change the number format for '**TTL**' columns to include a comma (zero decimal places)

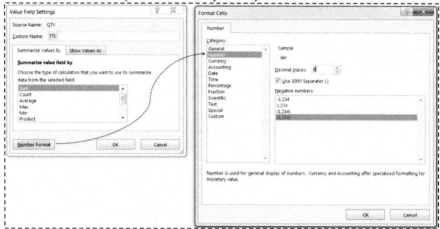

10. Click the '**Count of QTY2**' drop-down box and select '**Value Field Settings…**'
11. In the box '**Summarize value field by**' select '**Sum**'
12. In the field '**Custom Name:**' change to **+/-**

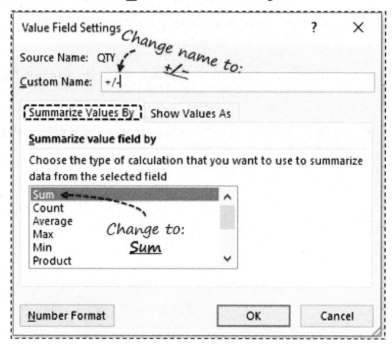

13. Select the tab '**Show Values As**'

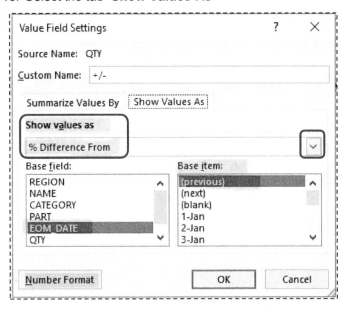

14. From the '**Show values as**' drop-down list select '**% Difference From**'

15. Select **Base field:** EOM_DATE & **Base item:** (previous)

16. Optionally, change the number format percent to one decimal place

17. Click the '**OK**' button

18. Change the label names:
    a. Change cell '**A28**' to **REGIONS**
    b. Change cell '**B26**' to **MONTH-YR**
    c. Change cell '**B28**' to **TTL**
    d. Change cell '**A33**' to **TOTAL**

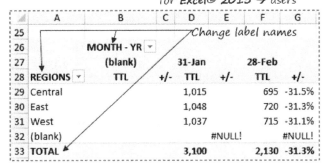

Formatting The Dashboard

We've added 3 of the 4 Pivot Tables for this Dashboard, before going further, let's format the tables to improve readability.

Due to page size limitations, the image of the entire Dashboard is not displayed:

	A	B	C	D	E	F	G	H
1								
2								
3	QUANTITY	CATEGORY ▼						
4	REGIONS ▼	FUEL	POWER	RUCTUR.	WING	(blank)	TOTAL	
5	Central	2,622	2,693	690	3,065		9,070	
6	East	2,541	2,700	696	3,051		8,988	
7	West	2,394	2,637	836	2,915		8,782	
8	(blank)							
9	TOTAL	7,557	8,030	2,222	9,031		26,840	
10								
11	)P 10 PARTS ▼	CATEGORY ▼	QTY SOLD	%				
12	Auxilliary Stru	WING	871	10.6%				
13	Boost Pumps	FUEL	789	9.6%				
14	Digital Fuel Fl	FUEL	783	9.5%				
15	Engine Lubric	FUEL	782	9.5%				
16	Engine Struts	WING	825	10.0%				
17	Fire Protectic	POWER	967	11.8%				
18	Fuel Dump Ft	FUEL	822	10.0%				
19	Keel Beam	STRUCTURAL	812	9.9%				
20	Spars	WING	772	9.4%				
21	Wing Webs	WING	791	9.6%				
22	TOTAL		8,214	100.0%				
23								
24								
25								
26		MONTH - YR ▼						
27		(blank)		31-Jan		28-Feb		31-Mar
28	REGIONS ▼	TTL	+/-	TTL	+/-	TTL	+/-	TTL
29	Central			1,015		695	-31.5%	991
30	East			1,048		720	-31.3%	945
31	West			1,037		715	-31.1%	945
32	(blank)				#NULL!		#NULL!	#N
33	TOTAL			3,100		2,130	-31.3%	2,881

Entire Dashboard shrunk to fit on book page:

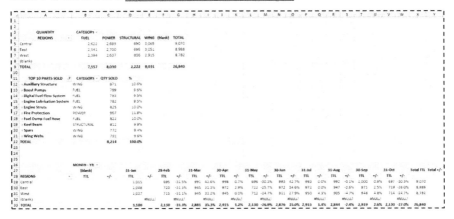

1. To change the display of formula error messages (such as #NULL!, #DIV/0!), select cell **'E32'**
2. From the **PivotTable Tools** Ribbon select the tab **Analyze**
3. Select the PivotTable drop-down box, then the **'Options'** drop-down box, then 'Op_t_ions'

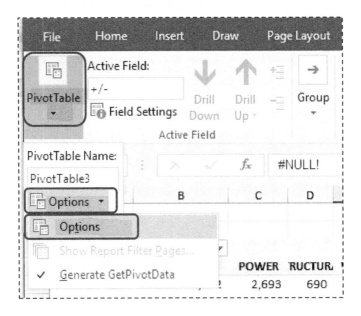

4. Under the '**Layout & Format**' tab, check the box '**For error values show:**'

5. Click the '**OK**' button

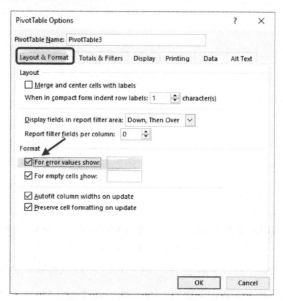

6. To filter out the (blank) columns and rows, select cell '**B3**' click the drop-down arrow and uncheck the **(blank)** field

7. Click the '**OK**' button
8. Repeat steps #6 & #7 for cell '**B11**' *(DO NOT REPEAT FOR CELL 'B26')*
9. Select cell '**X27**' **(Total TTL)**, **right-click** and select '**Remove Grand Total**'

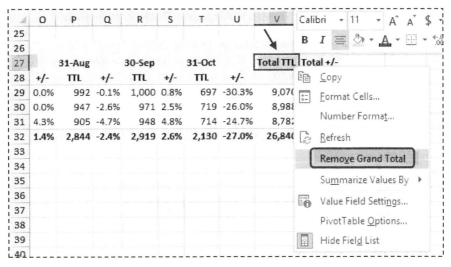

10. From the Ribbon select the '**VIEW**' tab and *uncheck* the '**Gridlines**' box

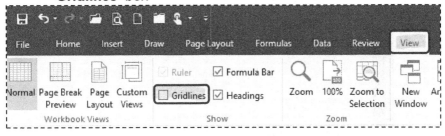

11. Click cell '**A3**', and then from the **PivotTable Tools** Ribbon select the tab **DESIGN : PivotTable Styles**

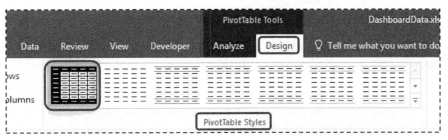

63

12. From the **PivotTable Styles** drop-down, select a format style you like
13. Repeat steps #11 & #12 for PivotTables in cells **'A11'** & **'A26'**
14. In cell **'A1'** enter the text **'Monthly Dashboard'**
15. In cell **'B1'** enter the text **'Airplane Parts by Region'**
16. Increase the font size of **'A1'** & **'B1'** to 18 and bold, *optionally you may change the font type to 'Consolas' and color of your choice*
17. **Right-click** on cell 'A3' and from the pop-up menu select **'PivotTable Options'**

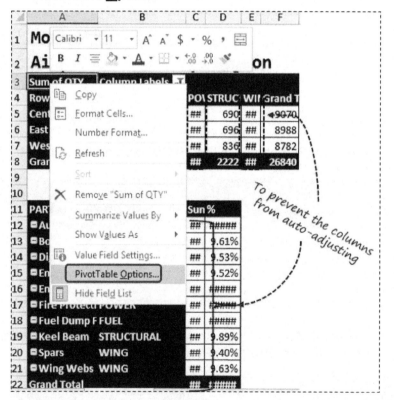

18. Under the **'Layout & Format'** tab, uncheck the box **'Autofit column widths on update'** *(see image on next page)*
19. Click the **'OK'** button
20. Repeat steps #17 - #19 for cells **'A11'** & **'A26'**
21. Then expand columns widths, so no # symbols display

Excel® Pivot Tables & Introduction To Dashboards
The Step-By-Step Guide

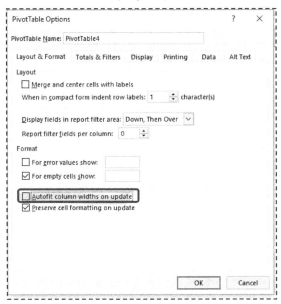

To change the sort order for the **'TOP 10 PARTS SOLD'** to descending

22. Click the drop-down box for cell **'A11'** and then **'More Sort Options…'**

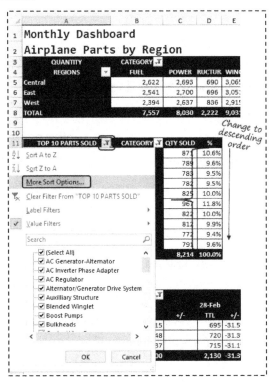

65

23. Select the **'Descending (Z to A) by:'** radio button
24. Click the drop-down box and the **'%'** option
25. Click the **'OK'** button

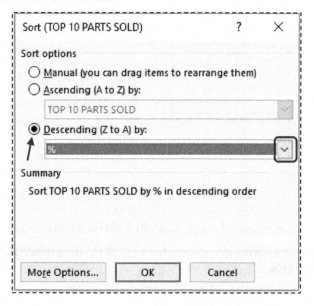

We're almost done! However, one of the trickiest *(and most frustrating)* aspects about formatting Pivot Tables is keeping the desired format **when new data is added**, especially when working with date values, in this case when new months are included. You'll learn more about adding data in chapter 9.

Meanwhile, in order to prepare our Dashboard to keep the formatting for all new data. Sometimes, we have to perform redundant and non-intuitive steps. Our preferred formatting for the monthly Pivot Table is as follows:

- Date displayed as MMM-YYYY (i.e. Jan-2017)
- The month and year centered over the columns **'TTL'** and **'+/-'**
- Hide the (blank) rows and columns

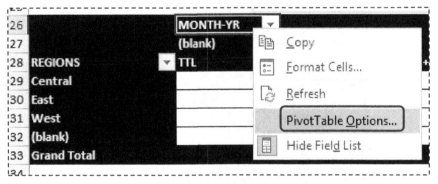

Because date Columns are dynamic, they require additional steps to keep formatting

When new months are added we want to keep this date format centered over both columns

26. **Right-click** cell **'B26'**

27. From the pop-up menu, select **'PivotTable Options'**

28. Under the **'Layout & Format'** tab, check the box **'Merge and center cells with labels'**

29. Click the **'OK'** button

To <u>apply the date format</u> we need to <u>ungroup</u> the field

Excel 2013 users may skip step #30

30. **Right-click** cell **'B27'**, from the pop-up menu, select **'Ungroup'**

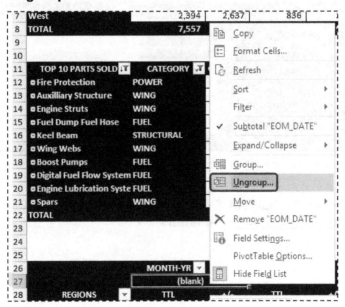

You'll notice when we did this our **'+/- percent'** column reverted back to the sum of quantity (in Excel® 2016 only). I assume Excel® did this because we ungrouped the field. Yet, it is still perplexing as to why it did not keep our **'Show values as'** commands. Therefore, we must re-apply steps #13 - #17 from page 59 to apply the **'+/- percent'** column.

I deliberated about structuring this lesson differently to avoid having to perform these redundant steps. However, I considered this to be a good example of some of the challenges you may experience when building Dashboards. Formatting glitches occur frequently. Don't be surprised if you find yourself spending a sizable amount of time addressing them.

	MONTH-YR	
REGIONS	1/31/2017	
	TTL	+/-
Central	1,015	1015
East	1,048	1048
West	1,037	1037
(blank)		
TOTAL	3,100	3100

After changing the **'+/- percent'** column back to display the **'% Difference From'** the previous month

31. Highlight cells **'B27:W27'** and **right-click** cell **'W27'**, from the pop-up menu, select **'Format Cells...'**

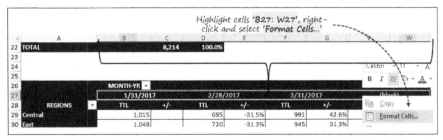

69

32. Under the '**Number**' tab select '**Custom**'
33. In the '**Type:**' field enter '**mmm-yyyy**'
34. Click the '**OK**' button

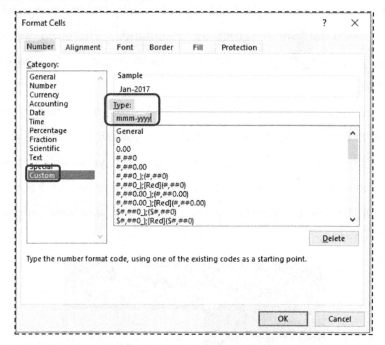

35. To filter out the (blank) columns and rows, select cell '**A28**' click the drop-down arrow and uncheck the **(blank)** field

36. Click the '**OK**' button

I know these formatting steps may have seemed onerous at times, but they have prepared our Dashboard to receive to new data and keep our existing formatting.

Due to page size limitations, some columns have been hidden:

Monthly Dashboard
Airplane Parts by Region

QUANTITY	CATEGORY				
REGIONS	FUEL	POWER	STRUCTURAL	WING	TOTAL
Central	2,622	2,693	690	3,065	9,070
East	2,541	2,700	696	3,051	8,988
West	2,394	2,637	836	2,915	8,782
TOTAL	7,557	8,030	2,222	9,031	26,840

TOP 10 PARTS SOLD	CATEGORY	QTY SOLD	%
Fire Protection	POWER	967	11.8%
Auxilliary Structure	WING	871	10.6%
Engine Struts	WING	825	10.0%
Fuel Dump Fuel Hose	FUEL	822	10.0%
Keel Beam	STRUCTURAL	812	9.9%
Wing Webs	WING	791	9.6%
Boost Pumps	FUEL	789	9.6%
Digital Fuel Flow System	FUEL	783	9.5%
Engine Lubrication Syste	FUEL	782	9.5%
Spars	WING	772	9.4%
TOTAL		8,214	100.0%

	MONTH-YR								
	Jan-2017		Feb-2017		Mar-2017		Oct-2017	
REGIONS	TTL	+/-	TTL	+/-	TTL	+/-	TTL	+/-
Central	1,015		695	-31.5%	991	42.6%	697	-30.3%
East	1,048		720	-31.3%	945	31.3%	719	-26.0%
West	1,037		715	-31.1%	945	32.2%	714	-24.7%
TOTAL	3,100		2,130	-31.3%	2,881	35.3%	2,130	-27.0%

Adding Charts To The Dashboard

Pie chart with the percent of total sales by region

To add our first chart we'll need to add another Pivot Table, however the customer has requested *only the pie chart and not the table displaying the percent of sales by region*. Therefore, we'll create the Pivot Table on a separate tab to save space and place only the pie chart on the Dashboard.

1. Return to the '**Data**' tab and highlight *columns* **A:F**
2. From the Ribbon select **INSERT : PivotTable**
3. Select the '**New Worksheet**' radio button
4. Click the '**OK**' button

A new tab will be created and the *'PivotTable Fields' pane* should appear on the left side of your screen.

5. Rename the tab from **'Sheet2'** *(you may be a different sheet#)* to **'PieChart'**

6. In the *'PivotTable Fields'* pane select the following fields:
    a. REGION *(Rows section)*
    b. QTY *(Values section)* **Please note: when adding the QTY fields, it will default to *'Count of QTY'*, change to *'Sum'***

7. Rename PivotTable to **'PieChart'**

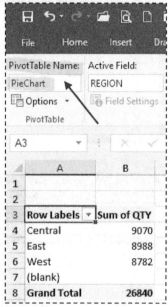

8. From the **PivotTable Tools** Ribbon select the tab **Analyze : PivotChart**

Excel® Pivot Tables & Introduction To Dashboards
The Step-By-Step Guide

9. The following prompt should be displayed, select the **'Pie'** option

10. Click the **'OK'** button

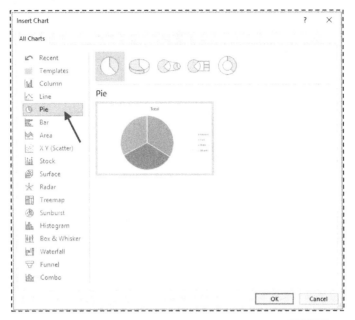

11. Click on the Pie chart and from the **PivotChart Tools** Ribbon select the tab **Design**

12. Click the drop-down for **'Quick Layout'** and then **'Layout 1'**

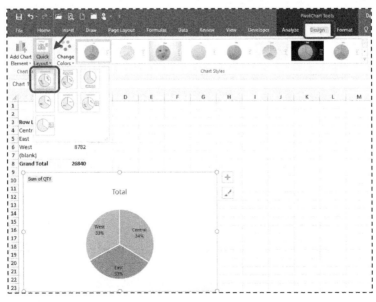

73

Optional steps: hide the Field buttons, **right-click** over any Field button and select the appropriate hide option. Remove the legend, by selecting the legend and pressing the delete key on your keyboard.

You may also change the color scheme, in this example I have chosen the first blue Monochromatic option

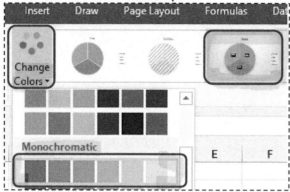

13. Change the chart title from **'Total'** to **'% of Sales by Region'**

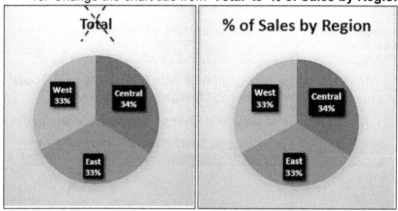

We'll now move the Pie chart to the Dashboard, by simply cutting and pasting.

14. Click on the Pie chart and press **(CTRL+X)** on your keyboard or:
    - From the Ribbon select the **'HOME'** tab
    - Click the **'Scissors'** icon

15. Click the **'Dashboard'** tab

16. Place your cursor in cell **'G3'** and press **(CTRL+V)** on your keyboard or:
    - From the Ribbon select the **'HOME'** tab

- Click the **'Paste'** button

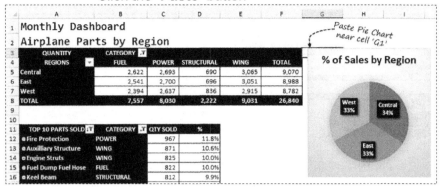

Lastly, we'll add the bar chart for 'quantity of parts sold by region and category':

17. On the **'Dashboard'** tab, click cell **'A3'**

18. From the **PivotTable Tools** Ribbon select the tab **Analyze : PivotChart**

19. The following prompt should be displayed, select the **'Bar'** option

20. Click the **'OK'** button

21. Drag the chart near cell **'L3'**

22. Rename Chart Name to **'BarChart'** *(see step #7 above)*

23. Click on the Bar chart and from the **PivotChart Tools** Ribbon select the tab **Design**

24. Click the drop-down for **'Quick Layout'** and then **'Layout 3'** *(see step #12 above)*

Optional steps: hide the Field buttons, **right-click** over any Field button and select the appropriate hide option

You may also change the color scheme, in this example I have chosen the black Monochromatic option

25. Change the chart title from **'Chart Title'** to **'Category Sales by Region'**

26. **Save** your Dashboard, you may keep the same filename or name to something different

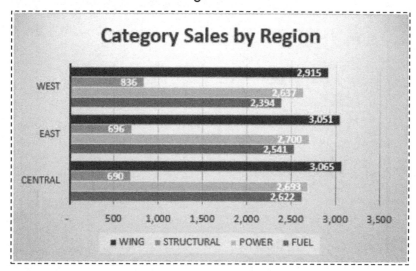

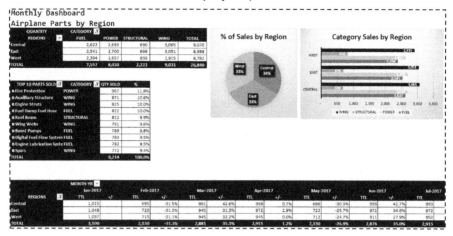

We've now fulfilled the customer requirements for delivering the Dashboard. To add additional functionality with slicers & performance symbols, please continue to chapter 8.

To learn about refreshing Pivot Table data see chapter 9 and to protect your Dashboard, please see chapter 10.

CHAPTER 8

Adding Slicers and Performance Symbols To Your Dashboard

In this chapter we explore two ways to enhance your Dashboard by using slicers and performance symbols. Building on the Dashboard we created in chapter 7 we will add:

1. A Timeline slicer
2. A Region slicer
3. Performance symbols (up / down arrows) to the sales by month Pivot Table

These enhancements will provide users with electronic or online access to the Dashboard the ability to examine the data by different time segments and regions. In addition to this, by adding symbols to indicate if sales were above or below the previous month, customers can quickly glance at the data and know how performance is trending, without the need to study the detail of the Pivot Table report.

Slicers

1. Open the Dashboard spreadsheet you created in chapter 7 and select **rows 3:6**
2. **Right-click** and from the pop-up menu select **'Insert'** *(4 blank rows, should now be added between the title and first Pivot Table)*
3. Click on cell **'A7'** and from the **PivotTable Tools** Ribbon select the tab **Analyze : Insert Timeline** *(for detailed instructions on how to insert a Timeline slicer please see chapter 6, page 33)*

Excel® Pivot Tables & Introduction To Dashboards
The Step-By-Step Guide

4. When prompted click the **'EOM_DATE'** checkbox
5. Click the **'OK'** button
6. A **Timeline slicer** should now appear, drag to the area near cell **'D1'**
7. **Right-click** on the newly added Timeline slicer and from the pop-up menu select **'Report Connections...'**

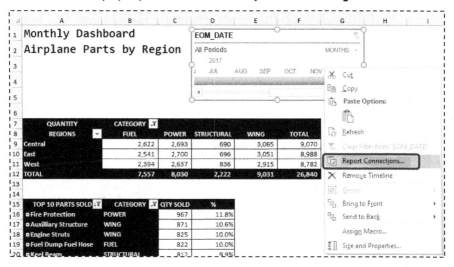

8. When prompted, select all checkboxes

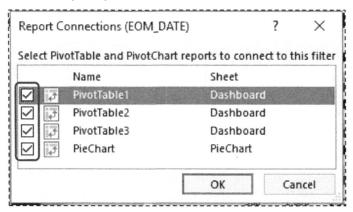

9. Click the **'OK'** button
10. From the **Timeline Tools** Ribbon under **'Options'** go to **'Caption'** and enter the new name of **'Time Frame'** *(for detailed instructions on how to change captions please see chapter 6 page 40)*

79

11. Click on cell **'A7'** and from the **PivotTable Tools** Ribbon select the tab **Analyze : Insert Slicer**

12. At the prompt click the **'REGION'** checkbox

13. Click the **'OK'** button

14. A new **slicer** should now appear, drag next to the Timeline slicer

15. **Right-click** on the newly added REGION slicer and from the pop-up menu select **'Slicer S**e**ttings…'**

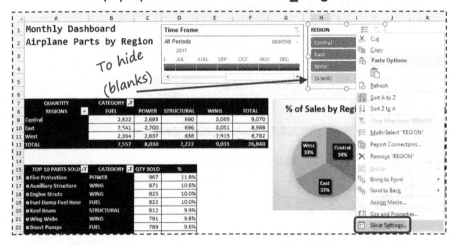

16. When prompted, check the box **'H**ide items with no data**'**

17. Click the **'OK'** button

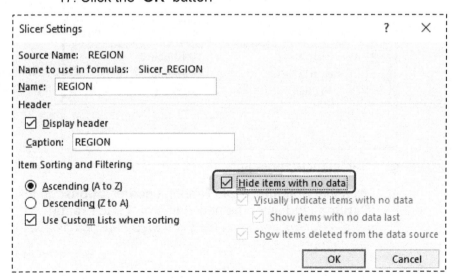

18. **Right-click** on the newly added region slicer and from the pop-up menu select **'Report Connections...'**

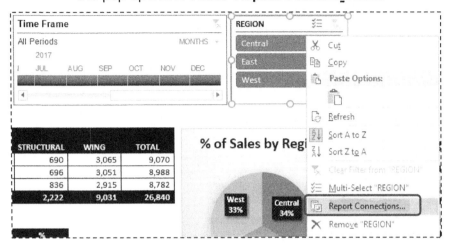

19. When prompted, select all checkboxes

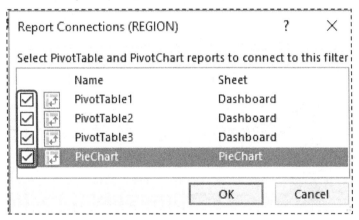

20. Click the **'OK'** button

Test the slicers by clicking on different combinations, you should see the Pivot Tables and charts expand and contract as you click.

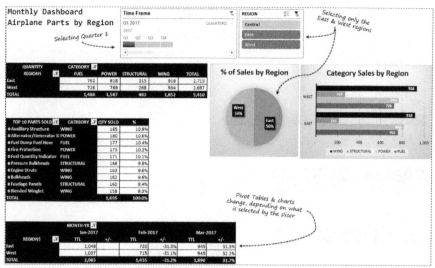

PLEASE NOTE!

Slicers *are filters*, when the 'Clear filter' button is selected any previous filters used, including those we applied **to hide (blank) columns & rows will be displayed.**

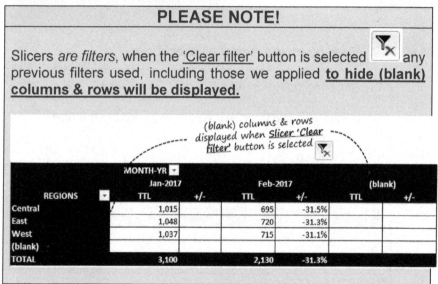

Performance Symbols (up/down arrows and other indicators)

1. Open the Dashboard spreadsheet you created in chapter 7 and **select all +/- columns** in the *'Quantity of parts sold by region and month'* Pivot Table.

    An easy way to accomplish this is by hovering your cursor near the line 'C32', **wait for the black down arrow** to appear and click so all +/- columns are now selected. *(See image below)*

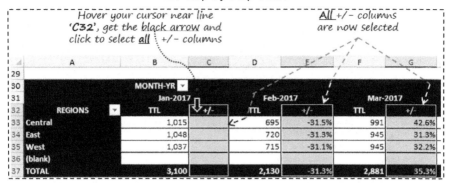

2. **With all +/- columns selected,** from the Ribbon select **HOME : Conditional Formatting** drop-down box

3. Select **'New Rule…'**

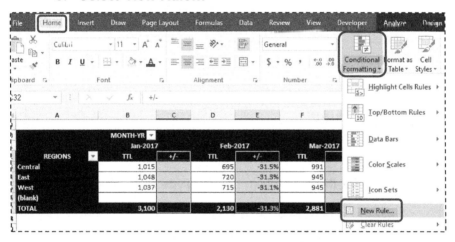

(See image below)

4. The following prompt will appear, select the radio button **'All cells showing "+/-" values'**

5. Click the drop-down box for **Format Style:** and select **'Icon Sets'**

6. Click the drop-down box for **Icon Style:** and *scroll-up* to select **the up/down arrows** ⬇ ➡ ⬆

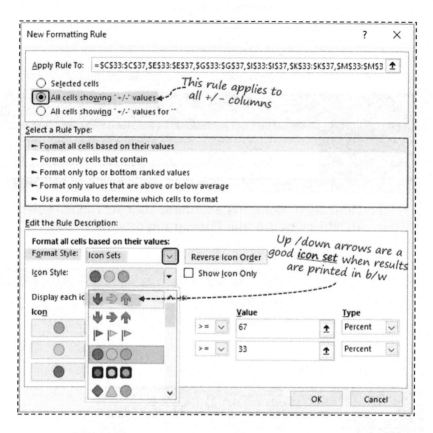

7. Click the drop-down box for **Type** and select **'Number'**

8. For the '**Values**' section enter:
   a. **0.000001** for 'when value is'
   b. **0** for 'when < 0.000001 and'

9. Click the 'OK' button

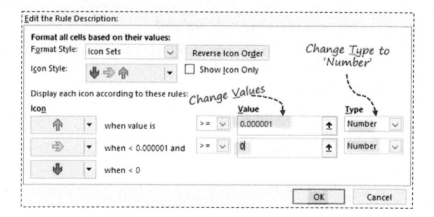

10. **Save** your Dashboard file

We now have performance symbols added to our Dashboard

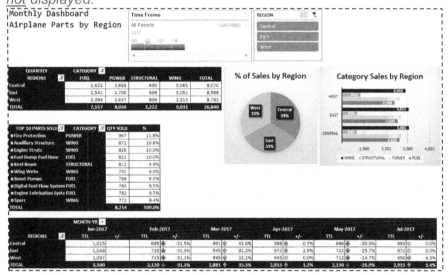

Due to page size limitations, the image of the entire Dashboard is not displayed:

We've now enhanced our Dashboard by using slicers and performance symbols.

To learn about refreshing Pivot Table data see chapter 9 and to protect your Dashboard, please see chapter 10.

CHAPTER 9
Refreshing Pivot Table and Dashboard Data

Once you have created a Pivot Table or Dashboard where the layout and format is to your liking and you receive new data, this new information may be added to your existing Pivot Table(s) by using the **Refresh** feature. By _refreshing your data, you may keep your current formatting and calculations_. Just remember in your initial design to allow for additional rows and columns that may be created when you're incorporating new data. Let's walk through an example.

1. Open the Dashboard spreadsheet you created in chapter 7
2. Click on any cell inside your first Pivot Table
3. From the **PivotTable Tools** Ribbon select the tab **Analyze**
4. Under **'PivotTable Name'** click the **'Options'** drop-down box and select **'Options'**

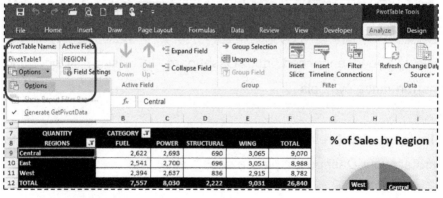

5. The following dialogue box will appear, select the **'Layout & Format'** tab

6. Verify the check box '**Preserve cell formatting on update**' is selected
7. Click the **'OK'** button

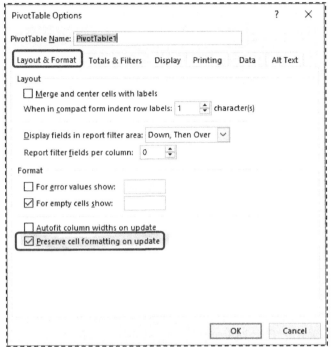

*Optionally, you may also click the check box '**Autofit column widths on update**'. I chose not to, I manually adjusted the columns to be the same width for each month. This is simply a design preference to give the Dashboard a more uniform look.*

8. **Repeat** steps #4 - #7 for each Pivot Table you've created

Verify your data source is correct

9. Select a cell in each PivotTable, from the **PivotTable Tools** Ribbon select the tab **Analyze**
10. Click the drop-down box **'Change Data Source'** and select **'Change Data Source…'**

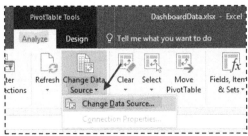

87

11. The following dialogue box will appear, verify the Table/Range is correct. In this case, since we'll be appending the data, selecting entire column is appropriate.

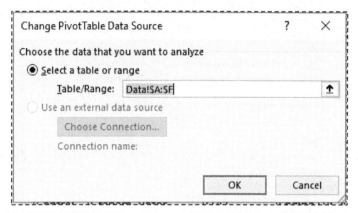

Note: you will **not** receive an error message if the **Range** is incorrect, however, the new data WILL NOT APPEAR in your Pivot Table / Dashboard.

12. Click the **'OK'** button

Next, we will add new data to the Dashboard

13. Click the **'Data'** tab

14. Select and **copy** cells **'H2:M649'** by pressing **(CTRL+C)** on your keyboard or:
    - From the Ribbon select the **'HOME'** tab
    - Click the **'Copy'** icon

15. Place your cursor in cell **'A3242'** and press **(CTRL+V)** on your keyboard or:
    - From the Ribbon select the **'HOME'** tab
    - Click the **'Paste'** button

	A	B	C	D	E	F
3239	West	Winchester, Charles	WING	Wing Attach Fitting	31 October 2017	7
3240	West	Winchester, Charles	WING	Engine Struts	31 October 2017	5
3241	West	Winchester, Charles	WING	Engine Mounts	31 October 2017	11
3242	Central	Graham, Peter	STRUCTURAL	Pressure Bulkheads	30 November 2017	16
3243	Central	Graham, Peter	STRUCTURAL	Keel Beam	30 November 2017	9
3244	Central	Graham, Peter	STRUCTURAL	Fuselage Panels	30 November 2017	9
3245	Central	Graham, Peter	FUEL	Boost Pumps	30 November 2017	16
3246	Central	Graham, Peter	FUEL	Transfer Valves	30 November 2017	9
3247	Central	Graham, Peter	FUEL	Fuel S.O.V.	30 November 2017	14
3248	Central	Graham, Peter	FUEL	Digital Fuel Flow System	30 November 2017	16

16. Return to the **'Dashboard' tab** and click on any cell inside your first Pivot Table
17. From the **PivotTable Tools** Ribbon select the tab **Analyze**
18. Click the drop-down box **'Refresh'** and select **'Refresh All'**

Refresh vs. Refresh All

Selecting the **'Refresh'** option would only update the **active** Pivot Table, by selecting **'Refresh All'** we're updating all of the Pivot Tables in the Dashboard.

We now have new data added to the Dashboard

Oct-2017		(blank)		Nov-2017		Dec-2017	
TTL	+/-	TTL	+/-	TTL	+/-	TTL	+/-
697 ⬇	-30.3%			1,081		1,296 ⬆	19.9%
719 ⬇	-26.0%			1,037		1,272 ⬆	22.7%
714 ⬇	-24.7%			999		1,252 ⬆	25.3%
2,130 ⬇	-27.0%			3,117		3,820 ⬆	22.6%

19. To address the **(blank)** column in our display, click on the drop-down box for **'MONTH-YR'** and select **'More Sort Options…**

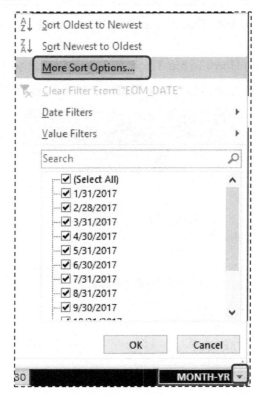

20. The following prompt will be displayed, select the **'Ascending (A to Z) by:'** radio button. From the drop-down box select **'EOM_DATE'**

21. Click the 'OK' button

Excel® Pivot Tables & Introduction To Dashboards
The Step-By-Step Guide

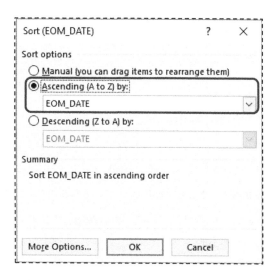

Our completed Dashboard:

Due to page size limitations, the image of the entire Dashboard is not displayed:

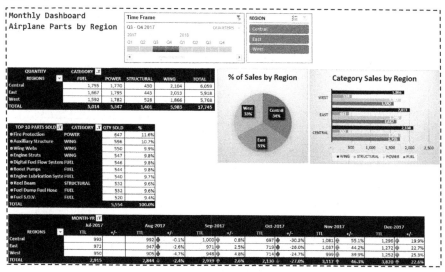

CHAPTER 10
Protecting Your Dashboard

Depending on your audience, you may want to consider *protecting* your Dashboard to prevent unauthorized users from modifying it. As well as, *hide* any data source tabs, allowing your customers to see only the Dashboard itself.

PLEASE NOTE!
Protecting **disables** the use of slicers and prevents users from manually refreshing the data.

Hiding Your Pivot Table Source Data

1. Open the Dashboard spreadsheet you created in chapter 7
2. To *hide* the 'PieChart' & 'Data' tabs, **right click** over the tabs and select '**H**ide' from the pop-up menu
3. To *unhide* **right click** over any tab and select '**U**nhide' *(the unhide option will become active once a tab is hidden)*

	A	B	C	D	E	F
3211	West	Winchester, Charles	FUEL	Fuel S.O.V.	31 October 2017	9
3212	West	Winchester, Charles	FUEL	Digital Fuel Flow System	31 October 2017	7
3213	West	Winchester, Charles	FUEL	Fuel Quantity Indicator	31 October 2017	3
3214	West	Winchester, Charles	FUEL	Fuel Flow Indicating	31 October 2017	4
3215	West	Winchester, Charles	FUEL	Fuel Pressure Indicating	31 October 2017	3
3216	West	Winchester, Charles	FUEL	Fuel Pump	31 October 2017	12
3217	West	Winchester, Charles	FUEL	Insert... em	31 October 2017	12
3218	West	Winchester, Charles	FUEL	Delete	31 October 2017	12
3219	West	Winchester, Charles	POWER	Rename	31 October 2017	8
3220	West	Winchester, Charles	POWER	Move or Copy... or	31 October 2017	4
3221	West	Winchester, Charles	POWER	View Code Drive System	31 October 2017	6
3222	West	Winchester, Charles	POWER	Protect Sheet... ation	31 October 2017	10
3223	West	*Right-Click over the tabs to receive the pop-up menu*		Tab Color	31 October 2017	10
3224	West				31 October 2017	10
3225	West			→ Hide	31 October 2017	2
3226	West			Unhide...	31 October 2017	4
3227	West	Winchester, Charles	POWER	Select All Sheets ter	31 October 2017	8
3228	West	Winchester, Charles	POWER	Ungroup Sheets	31 October 2017	8
3229	West	Winchester, Charles	POWER		31 October 2017	0

Dashboard | **PieChart** | Data

4. From the Ribbon select **Review : Protect Workbook**

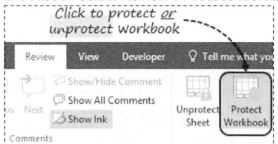

The following dialogue box will appear:

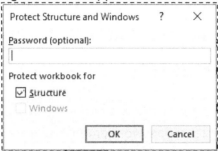

5. Optionally, enter a **Password** or leave blank
6. Click the **'OK'** button

Protecting The Dashboard Or Any Other Worksheet

1. From the Ribbon select **Review : Protect Sheet**

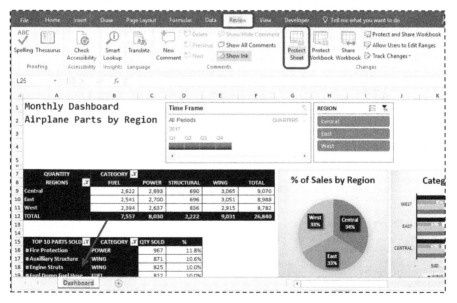

The following dialogue box will appear:

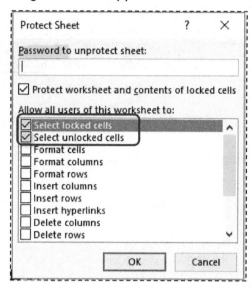

2. You may enter a password or leave blank
3. A good best practice is to leave the first two check boxes selected *(these will allow your customers to click on cells and scroll, but not change any content):*
   a. Select locked cells
   b. Select unlocked cells
4. Click the **'OK'** button

If a user tries to modify the sheet, they will receive the following message:

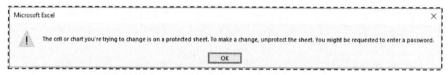

5. To **unprotect**, the sheet from the Ribbon select **Review : Unprotect Sheet**

CHAPTER 11

Grouping Pivot Table Data

In chapters 3 & 4 we reviewed different summary level types of analysis you can complete with Pivot Tables, however when you have a lot of detailed individual records such as customer demographics, sales, or location data. Sometimes more insight can be gained when you can cluster this data into categories or ranges. The **'Grouping'** feature allows you to complete this type of segmented analysis.

For example, let's say you received a large amount of *detailed* customer records and need to:

1. Group the number of customers by how much they spent
2. Include their groups percentage to the overall sales total for each segment

WEB ADDRESS & FILE NAME FOR EXERCISE:
http://bentonexcelbooks.my-free.website/excel-2016
CustomerSales.xlsx

Sample data for this chapter, due to space limitations **the entire data set is not displayed**.

	A	B
1	CUSTOMER ID	AMOUNT PURCHASED
2	111	$142
3	222	$153
4	333	$442
5	444	$409
6	555	$136
7	666	$147
8	777	$436
9	888	$403
10	999	$1,500
31	3330	$752

Grouping Records

Create a basic Pivot Table report, to see screenshot illustrations of steps #1 - #4, please see chapter 3 'Summarizing Numbers' page 7:

1. Open the CustomerSales.xlsx spreadsheet and highlight cells **A1:B31** *(select cells not columns)*
2. From the Ribbon select **INSERT : PivotTable**
3. Verify the '**New Worksheet**' radio button is selected
4. Click the '**OK**' button

A new tab will be created and the *'PivotTable Fields' pane* should appear on the left side of your screen.

5. Click the following fields:
   a. AMOUNT PURCHASE *(Rows section)*
   b. CUSTOMER ID *twice* *(Values section)*

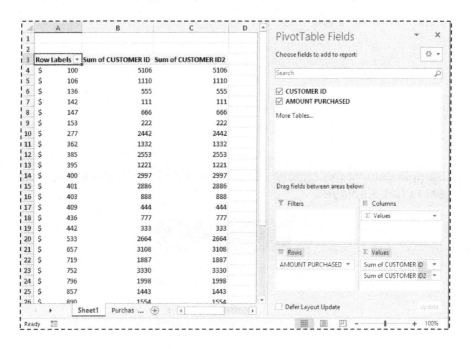

6. Click cell **'A4'**
7. From the **PivotTable Tools** Ribbon select the tab **Analyze : Group Field**

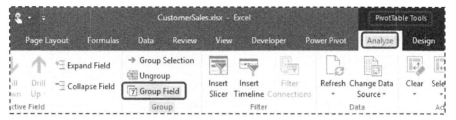

The following dialogue box will appear:

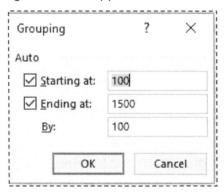

8. Verify both the **'Starting at:'** and **'Ending at:'** check boxes are selected

    - **'Starting at:'** will default to 100 (this is the *lowest value* in the dataset)
    - **'Ending at:'** will default to 1500 (this is the *highest value* in the dataset)

9. Enter 100 in the '**By:**' field *(this is the amount between group segments)*
10. Click the **'OK'** button

We've now grouped customer purchase amounts into segments, with each bracket differential representing approximately 100:

However, this table is not providing meaningful information, because it is incorrectly summing **'CUSTOMER ID'**, to fix this:

Row Labels	Sum of CUSTOMER ID	Sum of CUSTOMER ID2
100-199	7770	7770
200-299	2442	2442
300-399	5106	5106
400-499	8325	8325
500-599	2664	2664
600-699	3108	3108
700-799	7215	7215
800-899	2997	2997
900-999	3219	3219
1000-1099	4329	4329
1100-1199	3441	3441
1400-1500	999	999
Grand Total	51615	51615

Purchase Segments

Incorrectly Summing Customer ID

11. In the PivotTable Fields list, in the **'VALUES'** section, click the drop-down box for **'Sum of CUSTOMER ID'**

12. Select the **'Value Field Settings…'** option

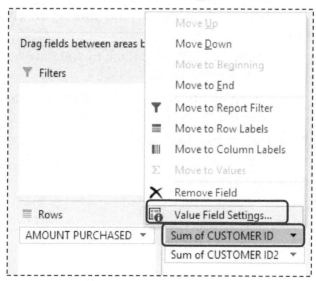

Count Function

The following dialogue box will appear:

13. In the '**Summarize value field by'** list box select **'Count'**

14. In the **'Custom Name:'** field change to '**NUMBER OF CUSTOMERS'**

15. Click the **'OK'** button

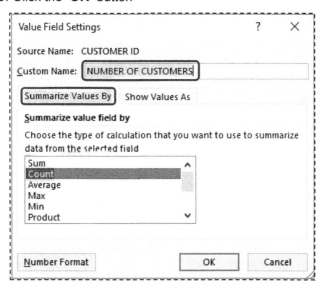

16. In the **PivotTable Fields** list, in the **'VALUES'** section, click the drop-down box **'Sum of CUSTOMER ID2'**

17. Select the **'Value Field Settings...'** option

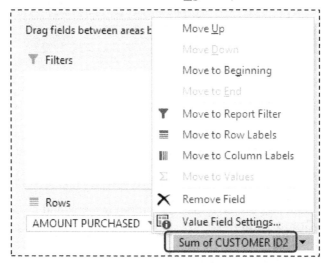

18. In the **'Summarize value field by'** list select **'Count'**
19. In the **'Custom Name:'** field change to '**% OF CUSTOMERS**'

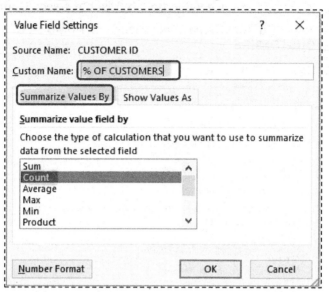

20. Click the **'Show Values As'** tab

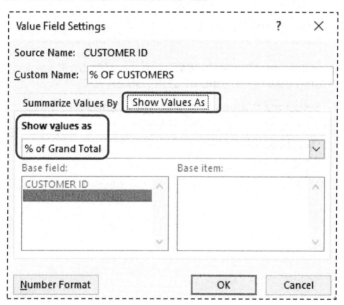

21. Click the **'Show values as'** drop-down box and select **'% of Grand Total'**

22. Click the **'OK'** button
23. Change the text in cell **'A3'** form "Row Labels" to **'AMOUNT PURCHASED'**

We now have a report that groups the number of customers by how much they spent and the segment's percentage to the overall sales total.

	AMOUNT PURCHASED	NUMBER OF CUSTOMERS	% OF CUSTOMERS
3			
4	100-199	7	23.33%
5	200-299	1	3.33%
6	300-399	3	10.00%
7	400-499	6	20.00%
8	500-599	1	3.33%
9	600-699	1	3.33%
10	700-799	3	10.00%
11	800-899	2	6.67%
12	900-999	1	3.33%
13	1000-1099	2	6.67%
14	1100-1199	2	6.67%
15	1400-1500	1	3.33%
16	Grand Total	30	100.00%

CHAPTER 12

Calculated Fields In Pivot Tables

As demonstrated in previous chapters, Pivot Tables have many powerful analysis features already built-in, however the type of work you perform may require more complex or technical types of calculations than those included in the standard set of Pivot Table **'Value Field Settings.'** This is when the ability to insert your own **'Calculated Fields'** is particularly helpful.

For example, let's say you're responsible for analyzing your company's sales location plan vs. actual. In addition to this you also determine if a store is eligible for a bonus and *if* they earned a bonus what the bonus amount is to be paid.

You perform this type of analysis on a regular basis and it is the type of business, where some *stores may close and others open from month-to-month.* You need to report:

A. The monthly sales dollar variance -/+ plan vs. actual by location

B. The monthly percent variance -/+ plan vs. actual by location

C. If the store is eligible for a bonus, based on actual sales greater than 1.5% over planned sales

D. If the store earned a bonus, the dollar amount owed to each location, which is 2% of that store's actual sales

WEB ADDRESS & FILE NAME FOR EXERCISE:
http://bentonexcelbooks.my-free.website/excel-2016
StoresSales.xlsx

Excel® Pivot Tables & Introduction To Dashboards
The Step-By-Step Guide

Sample data for this chapter:

	A	B	C	D	E	F	G	H	I
1	Location	Month	Planned Sales	Actual Sales					
2	AAA	Jan	406	414		AAA	Apr	432	450
3	BBB	Jan	332	329		BBB	Apr	338	329
4	CCC	Jan	496	526		CCC	Apr	509	526
5	DDD	Jan	152	156		DDD	Apr	155	150
6	EEE	Jan	178	173		FFF	Apr	191	170
7	AAA	Feb	415	427		GGG	Apr	181	170
8	BBB	Feb	346	342					
9	CCC	Feb	551	595					
10	DDD	Feb	175	184					
11	EEE	Feb	173	183					
12	AAA	Mar	424	416					
13	BBB	Mar	360	363					
14	CCC	Mar	612	648					
15	DDD	Mar	202	207					
16	EEE	Mar	168	163					

Adding A Basic Calculated Field

Create a basic Pivot Table report, to see screenshot illustrations of steps #1 - #4, please see chapter 3 'Summarizing Numbers' page 7:

1. Open the StoreSales.xlsx spreadsheet and highlight **columns A:D**
2. From the Ribbon select **INSERT : PivotTable**
3. Select the '**New Worksheet**' radio button
4. Click the '**OK**' button

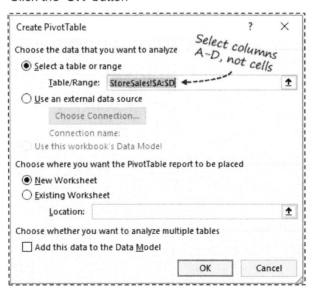

103

C.J. Benton

A new tab will be created and the *'PivotTable Fields' pane* should appear on the left side of your screen.

5. Select the following fields:
   a. Location *(Columns section)*
   b. Month *(Rows section)*
   c. Planned Sales and Actual Sales *(Values section)*) **Please note: when adding the QTY fields, it will default to 'Count of QTY', change to 'Sum'**
   d. ∑ Value *(Rows section)* – drag this field to the rows section

[Pivot table screenshot showing Row Labels with Jan, Feb, Mar sections containing Sum of Planned Sales and Sum of Actual Sales, with Column Labels AAA, BBB, CCC, DDD, EEE, (blank), Grand Total. PivotTable Fields pane on right with Location, Month, Planned Sales, Actual Sales checked. Note: "Make sure the 'Σ Values' field is *after* the 'Month' field"]

6. Change the text in cell **'A4'** to **'MONTH'**

7. Change the text in cell **'B3'** to **'LOCATION'**

8. For **'Sum of Planned Sales'** under **'Value Field Settings'**
   - Change the name to **'PLN SLS'**
   - The **'Number Format'** to a *currency* of your choice

9. For **'Sum of Actual Sales'** under **'Value Field Settings'**
   - Change the name to **'ACT SLS'**
   - The **'Number Format'** to a *currency* of your choice

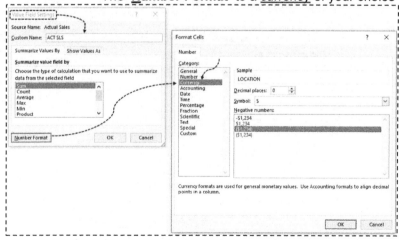

104

The Pivot Table should look *similar* to the following:

MONTH	LOCATION						
	AAA	BBB	CCC	DDD	EEE	(blank)	Grand Total
Jan							
PLN SLS	$406	$332	$496	$152	$178		$1,564
ACT SLS	$414	$329	$526	$156	$173		$1,598
Feb							
PLN SLS	$415	$346	$551	$175	$173		$1,660
ACT SLS	$427	$342	$595	$184	$183		$1,731
Mar							
PLN SLS	$424	$360	$612	$202	$168		$1,766
ACT SLS	$416	$363	$648	$207	$163		$1,797
(blank)							
PLN SLS							
ACT SLS							
Total PLN SLS	$1,245	$1,038	$1,659	$529	$519		$4,990
Total ACT SLS	$1,257	$1,034	$1,769	$547	$519		$5,126

We'll hide the (blank) fields in a later step

To add our first calculated field showing the sales dollar variance -/+ plan vs. actual.

    10. From the **PivotTable Tools** Ribbon select the tab **Analyze**

    11. Click the **'Fields, Items & Sets'** drop-down box

    12. Select **'Calculated Field…'**

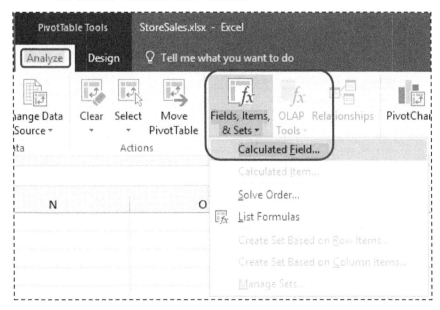

The following dialogue box will appear:

13. In the **Name:** field enter '**Dollars -/+ plan vs actual**'

14. In the **Formula:** field delete the zero '0', but leave the equal '=' sign

15. Select **'Actual Sales'** from the '**Fields**' list and click the '**Insert Field**' button

16. Add the minus '-' symbol in the **Formula:** field after **'Actual Sales'**

17. Select **'Planned Sales'** from the '**Fields**' list and click the '**Insert Field**' button

The following formula should now be in the '**Formula:**' field

='ACTUAL SALES' -'PLAN SALES'

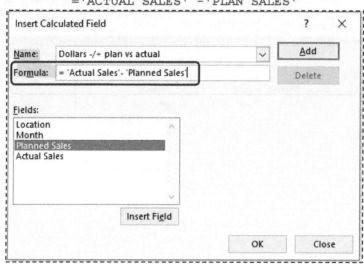

106

18. Click the **'OK'** button

The following field was added to our PivotTable results:

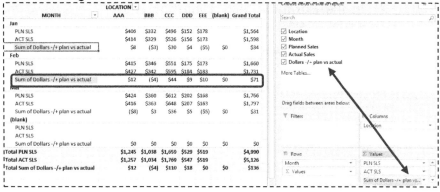

Next, we'll add the calculated field for the percent variance -/+ plan vs. actual

19. Repeat steps# 10 – 12 from above

The following dialogue box will appear:

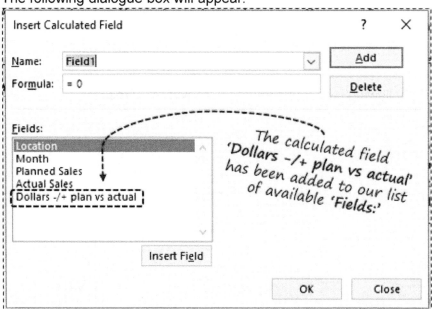

20. In the **Name:** field enter **'Percent -/+ plan vs actual'**

21. In the **Formula:** field delete the zero '0', but leave the equal '=' sign

22. Add the below formula to the **Formula:** field
    =('Actual Sales'-'Planned Sales')/ 'Planned Sales'

23. Click the **'OK'** button

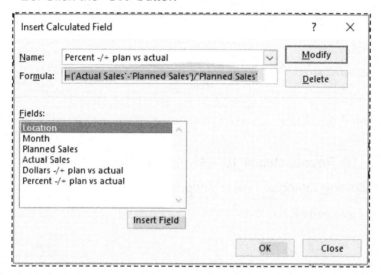

The following field was added to our PivotTable results:

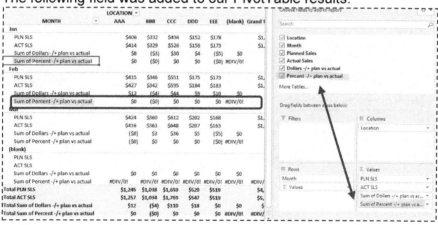

Let's now format our report to improve readability

1. In the PivotTable Fields list, in the **'VALUES'** section, click the drop-down box for **'Sum of Dollars -/+ plan vs actual'**

2. Select the **'Value Field Settings…'**

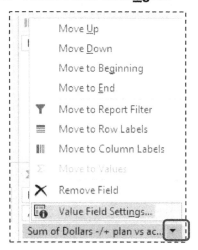

3. Change the '**C**ustom Name:' to **'$ -/+ PLN vs. ACT'**
4. Click the **'OK'** button

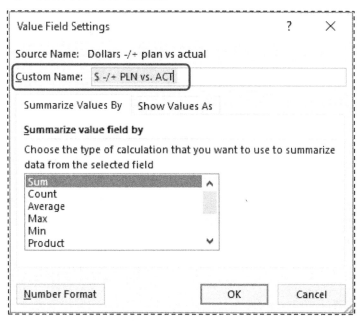

5. In the PivotTable Fields list, in the **'VALUES'** section, click the drop-down box for **'Sum of Percent -/+ plan vs actual'**
6. Select the **'Value Field Settings…'**
7. Change the '**C**ustom Name:' to **"% -/+ PLN vs. ACT"**

8. Click the **'Number Format'** to change the format to a percentage with 1 decimal place

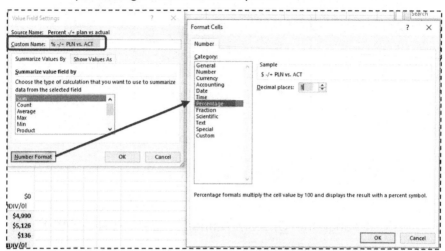

9. Click the **'OK'** button for each dialogue box
10. Click the drop-down box for **'MONTH'** and select **'Label Filters'** then **'Does Not Equal…'**

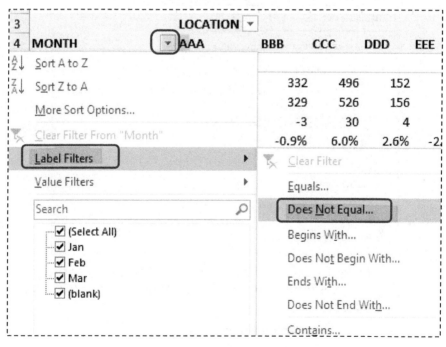

11. When prompted enter **(blank)**, *this method will ensure when we refresh the data, the blank rows & columns will not appear, but our new locations will.*

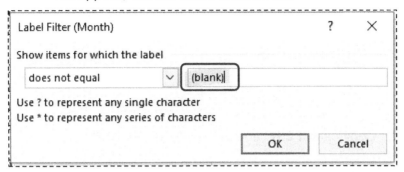

12. From the **PivotTable Tools** Ribbon select the tab **Design**
13. Select **'PivotTable Style'** of your choice
14. Click the checkbox **'Banded Columns'**

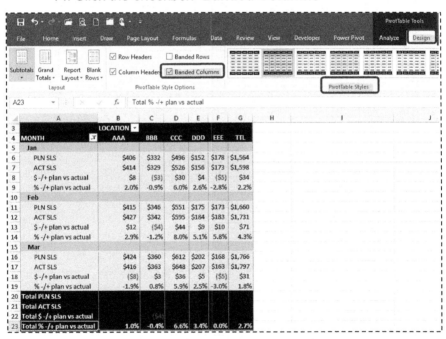

Now let's examine how our results change when we *add* or *remove* locations.

1. Return to the **'StoreSales'** tab

111

2. Copy cells **'F2:I7'** and paste into in cell **'A17'**

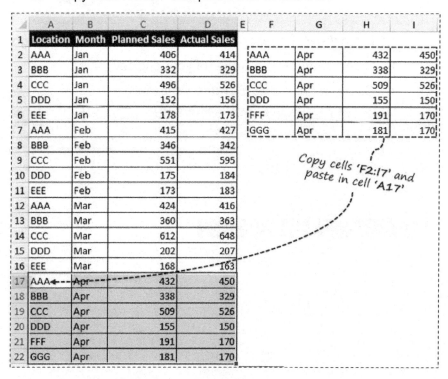

3. Return to the **Pivot Tables** tab, from the **PivotTable Tools** Ribbon select the tab **Analyze**

4. Click **'Refresh : Refresh All'**

Changing The Display Of Formula Error Messages

A report similar to the following should now appear:

	A	B	C	D	E	F	G	H	I
3		**LOCATION**							
4	**MONTH**	**AAA**	**BBB**	**CCC**	**DDD**	**EEE**	**FFF**	**GGG**	**TTL**
5	**Jan**								
6	PLN SLS	$406	$332	$496	$152	$178			$1,564
7	ACT SLS	$414	$329	$526	$156	$173			$1,598
8	$ -/+ plan vs actual	$8	($3)	$30	$4	($5)	$0	$0	$34
9	% -/+ plan vs actual	2.0%	-0.9%	6.0%	2.6%	-2.8%	#DIV/0!	#DIV/0!	2.2%
10	**Feb**								
11	PLN SLS	$415	$346	$551	$175	$173			$1,660
12	ACT SLS	$427	$342	$595	$184	$183			$1,731
13	$ -/+ plan vs actual	$12	($4)	$44	$9	$10	$0	$0	$71
14	% -/+ plan vs actual	2.9%	-1.2%	8.0%	5.1%	5.8%	#DIV/0!	#DIV/0!	4.3%
15	**Mar**								
16	PLN SLS	$424	$360	$612	$202	$168			$1,766
17	ACT SLS	$416	$363	$648	$207	$163			$1,797
18	$ -/+ plan vs actual	($8)	$3	$36	$5	($5)	$0	$0	$31
19	% -/+ plan vs actual	-1.9%	0.8%	5.9%	2.5%	-3.0%	#DIV/0!	#DIV/0!	1.8%
20	**Apr**								
21	PLN SLS	$432	$338	$509	$155		$191	$181	$1,806
22	ACT SLS	$450	$329	$526	$150		$170	$170	$1,795
23	$ -/+ plan vs actual	$18	($9)	$17	($5)	$0	($21)	($11)	($11)
24	% -/+ plan vs actual	4.2%	-2.7%	3.3%	-3.2%	#DIV/0!	-11.0%	-6.1%	-0.6%
25	**Total PLN SLS**								
26	**Total ACT SLS**								
27	**Total $ -/+ plan vs actual**		($11)				($21)	($11)	
28	**Total % -/+ plan vs actual**	1.8%	-0.9%	5.9%	1.9%	0.0%	-11.0%	-6.1%	1.8%

5. To remove the #DIV/0! display, select the **'Options'** drop-down box, then '**Op_tions**'

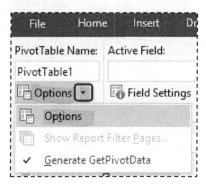

6. Under the **'Layout & Format'** tab, check the box **'For error values show:'**
7. Click the **'OK'** button

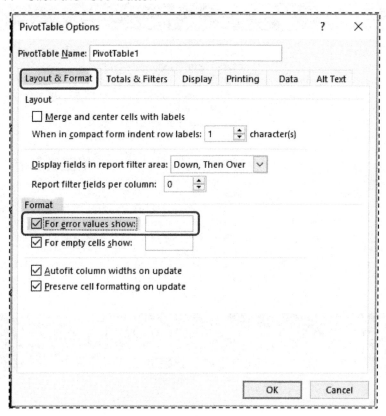

Removing Or Changing Calculated Fields

To remove or change a calculated field:

1. From the **PivotTable Tools** Ribbon select the tab **Analyze**
2. Click the **'Fields, Items & Sets'** drop-down box
3. Select **'Calculated Field...'**

The following dialogue box will appear:

4. In the **'Name:'** drop-down box select the calculated field you would like to change or remove
5. Click appropriate button, either **'Modify'** or **'Delete'**

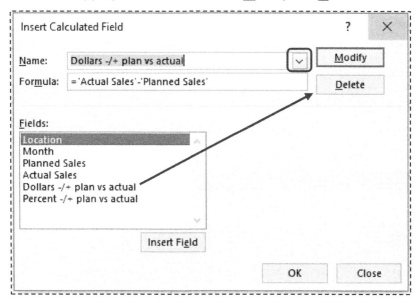

Inserting Logic Fields *(if...then)*

We'll need to add two additional calculated fields, in order to answer the following questions:

- Is the store eligible for a bonus based on actual sales greater than 1.5% over planned sales?
- If the store earned a bonus, what is the dollar amount owed to that location? *This is calculated as 2% of that store's actual sales.*

The two calculated fields needed:

A. <u>Location Eligibility Amount</u> to calculate what is 1.5% over the planned sales for each location?

B. <u>Bonus Award</u> the dollar amount owed, *if* they earned the bonus, what is 2% of actual sales for that location?

Location_Eligibility_Amt formula:

='Planned Sales'+('Planned Sales'*0.015)

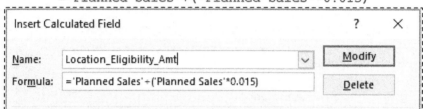

Bonus_Award formula:

=IF('Actual Sales'>Location_Eligibility_Amt,('Actual Sales'*0.02),0)

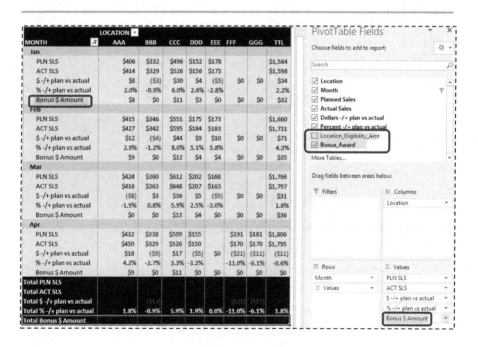

CHAPTER 13

Creating Pivot Tables From Imported Files – using the Data Model

Like with many tasks in Excel®, file importing and parsing can be accomplished in multiple ways. The following example describes how to read and parse a .CSV (comma separated value) file using Excel's® Data Model technique. Then applying the parsed data to create a Pivot Table report.

The Excel® Data Model is a feature in which different data sources can be brought together into a single workbook. Once this information is in the workbook, you're able to create more robust Pivot Tables, Pivot Charts, or Power View reports.

This type of reporting can also be achieved by using macros (Visual Basic for Applications) or Power Pivot. Deciding which method to use depends a on variety of factors, such as:

- The amount of data your analyzing
- The complexity and time it takes to complete your analysis
- Your audience's requirements
- Your experience with Excel®

In the following example, the reporting is straightforward, we'll be reporting on less than 100 records. Our Excel® Data Model will contain only one data source.

In this example, you're a Business Analyst and a request has been made to change a monthly employee sales report. Management would now like to see:

A. A regional summary
B. Employee sales grouped and subtotaled by region

Employee sales are captured in a legacy system. This older system produces a monthly *.CSV file* and saves it to a company server location. To save time formatting the same report each month you create Pivot Tables to parse the .CSV file and format the data into a Excel® report.

WEB ADDRESS & FILE NAMES FOR EXERCISE:
http://bentonexcelbooks.my-free.website/excel-2016
EmployeeSales.csv

ADDITIONAL STEP FOR THIS CHAPTER

Save the **EmployeeSales.csv** file to a location on your computer you can easily access such as a temporary folder or your desktop.

EXAMPLE:
From:

Excel® Pivot Tables & Introduction To Dashboards
The Step-By-Step Guide

To:

	A	B	C D	E	F
1	Employee & Region Sales Report				
2					
3	**EMPLOYEE & REGION**	**MONTH** ▼		**REGION**	**MONTH** ▼
4	**SALES** ▼	March		**SALES** ▼	March
5	⊟ **Central**	**19,054**		Central	19,054
6	Becker	4,647		East	13,769
7	Johnson	4,386		South	20,979
8	Morton	3,425		West	16,887
9	Smith	3,370		**TOTAL**	**70,689**
10	Taylor	3,226			
11	⊟ **East**	**13,769**			
12	Dower	3,871			
13	Nelson	3,117			
14	Taylor	3,752			
15	Wilson	3,029			
16	⊟ **South**	**20,979**			
17	Bates	3,834			
18	Blatchford	4,350			
19	Campbell	4,285			
20	Lewis	4,805			
21	Tansae	3,705			
22	⊟ **West**	**16,887**			
23	Graham	4,456			
24	Smith	4,787			
25	Tanner	4,520			
26	Williams	3,124			
27	**TOTAL**	**70,689**			

---

1. Create a new blank Excel® spreadsheet **(CTRL + N)**
2. Rename **'Sheet1'** to **'Monthly Sales Report'**
3. Select cell **'A1'** and enter the text **'Employee & Region Sales Report'**
4. Select cell **'A3'**
5. From the Ribbon select **INSERT** : **PivotTable**

119

The following dialogue box will appear:

6. Select the **'Use an external data source'** radio button
7. Click the **'Add this data to the Data Model'** checkbox

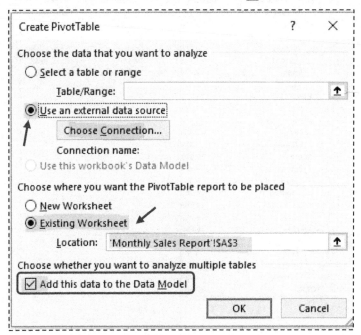

8. Click the **'Choose Connection…'** button

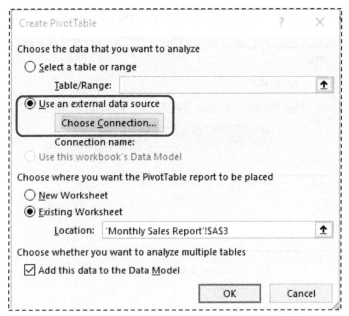

A prompt *similar* to the following should appear:

9. Click the **'Browse for More…'** button
10. When prompted select the file path where the file **'EmployeeSales.csv'** is located
11. Click the **'Open'** button

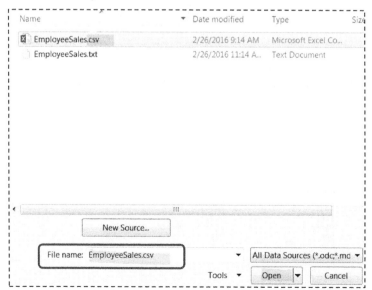

The following **Text Import Wizard** will be displayed:

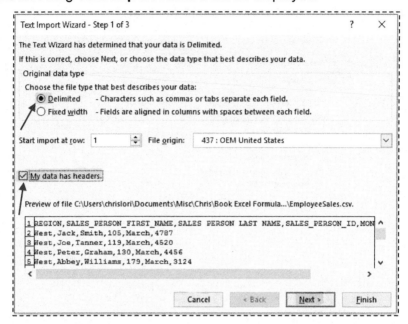

12. Select the **'Delimited'** radio button and **'My data has headers'** check box

13. Click the **'Next>'** button

Step 2 of the **Text Import Wizard** will be displayed:

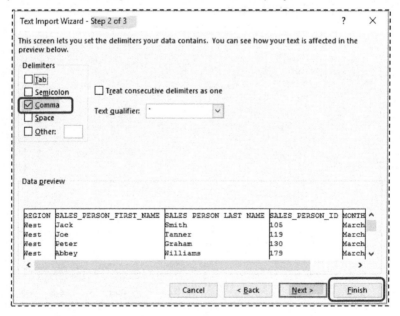

14. For the Delimiters, select the **'Comma'** check box

15. Click the **'Finish'** button

The following prompt will appear:

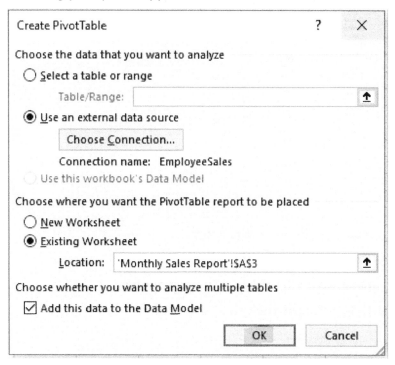

16. Click the **'OK'** button

A prompt similar to the following should appear *(it may take moment to load)*:

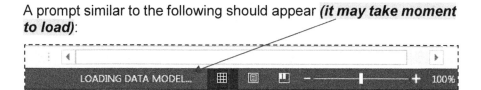

17. In the *'PivotTable Fields'* pane select the following fields:
    - REGION &SALES PERSON LAST NAME *(Rows section)*
    - MONTH *(Columns section)*
    - SALES *(Values section)*

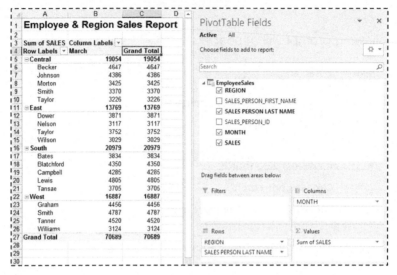

18. Place your cursor in cell **'E3'**

19. Repeat steps 5 – 8 from above

A prompt similar to the following should appear:

20. Select **'EmployeeSales'** and click the **'Open'** button

21. Click the **'OK'** button

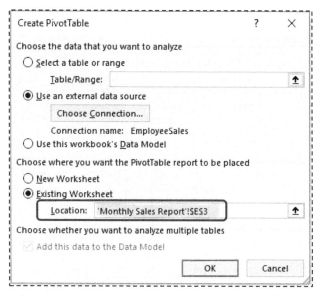

22. In the *'PivotTable Fields'* pane select the following fields:
    - REGION *(Rows section)*
    - MONTH *(Columns section)*
    - SALES *(Values section)*

23. **Right-click** over *both* **'Grand Total'** fields and select **'Remove Grand Total'**

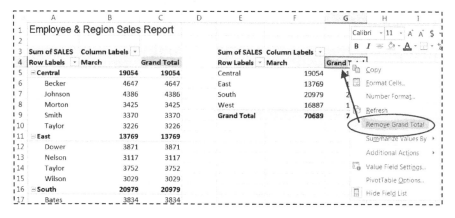

125

24. Re-label and format column headings, change currency to your preference

CHAPTER 14

Troubleshooting: Pivot Tables Displaying Duplicate Values

Sometimes the data we're analyzing is not in a format conducive for Pivot Tables. Cell values may contain extra spaces between and after words. This can cause Pivot Table reports to display incorrect results, below are two examples of this issue and how to resolve them.

WEB ADDRESS & FILE NAME FOR EXERCISE:
http://bentonexcelbooks.my-free.website/excel-2016
FormulasLenAndTrim.xlsx

Example:

You've been given an report that was created by a Data Base Administrator (DBA). The DBA created the file by running a query in a database, exporting the results into a .CSV file, and then opened and re-saved the report as an Excel® file.

As the Business Analyst, you're attempting to reconcile the data using a Pivot Table. In your analysis, you've discovered cell values that *"look"* to be the same, but are being returned as two separate records in your results.

You decide to use the **LEN function** to troubleshoot why you're getting two separate records in your results for what appear to be the same value.

Below is an illustration of the Pivot Table report showing the incorrect values.

Formula - LEN

Definition: The LEN formula counts the number characters in a cell

```
Formula Syntax:
LEN(text)
text is required
```

1. Open the FormulasLenAndTrim.xlsx spreadsheet
2. Select the tab named **'Len'**

3. Sorting the results by **'Fruit Name'** in <u>**Ascending order**</u>

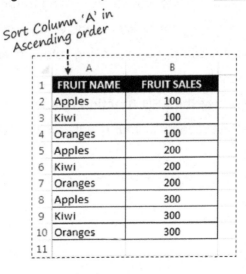

4. Select cell '**C1**' and label it "**LEN FUNCTION**"
5. Click cell '**C2**'

	A	B	C
1	FRUIT NAME	FRUIT SALES	LEN FUNCTION
2	Apples	100	
3	Apples	200	
4	Apples	300	
5	Kiwi	100	
6	Kiwi	200	
7	Kiwi	300	
8	Oranges	100	
9	Oranges	200	
10	Oranges	300	
11			

6. From the Ribbon select **Formulas : Text : LEN**

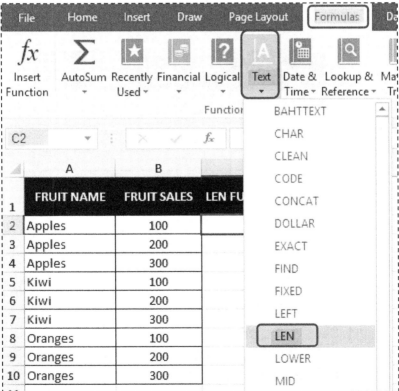

The following dialogue box will appear:

7. Click on cell '**A2**' or enter '**A2**' in the **Text** field
8. Click the '**OK**' button

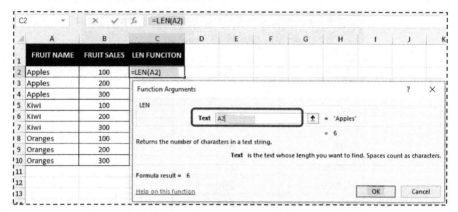

9. Copy the LEN formula down to cells '**C3**' thru '**C10**'

There appears to be an extra space in cells '**A3**' & '**A4**' after the fruit name '*Apple*'

	A	B	C
1	FRUIT NAME	FRUIT SALES	LEN FUNCTION
2	Apples	100	6
3	Apples	200	7
4	Apples	300	7
5	Kiwi	100	4
6	Kiwi	200	4
7	Kiwi	300	4
8	Oranges	100	7
9	Oranges	200	7
10	Oranges	300	7

10. Remove the extra space in cells '**A3** & **A4**' for the fruit name 'Apple'
11. Save your changes
12. You would now be able to re-run your Pivot Table report and results should appear correctly

	A	B
3	Row Labels	Sum of FRUIT SALES
4	Apples	600
5	Kiwi	600
6	Oranges	600
7	Grand Total	1800

Example:

You've been given a Excel® report generated by another application. Upon review you see the content in the cells contains extra spaces between and after the words. In order to make the report usable for analysis and presentation you need to remove the extraneous spaces. You decide to use the **TRIM function** to remove the spaces.

Below is an example of the report showing that must be corrected in order to create a Pivot Table report.

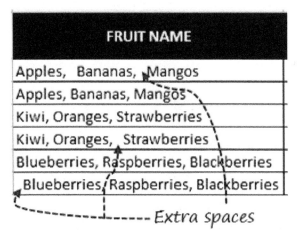

Formula - TRIM

Definition: Removes all extraneous spaces from a cell, except for single spaces between words.

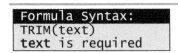

1. Open the FormulasLenAndTrim.xlsx spreadsheet

2. Select the tab named **'Trim'**

3. Click cell '**C2**'

	A	B	C
1	FRUIT NAME	LEN COUNT OF CHARACTERS	TRIM FUNCTION
2	Apples, Bananas, Mangos	27	
3	Apples, Bananas, Mangos	23	
4	Kiwi, Oranges, Strawberries	27	
5	Kiwi, Oranges, Strawberries	29	
6	Blueberries, Raspberries, Blackberries	38	
7	Blueberries, Raspberries, Blackberries	40	

4. From the Ribbon select **Formulas : Text : TRIM**

The following dialogue box will appear:

5. Click cell '**A2**' or enter '**A2**' in the **Text** field
6. Click the '**OK**' button

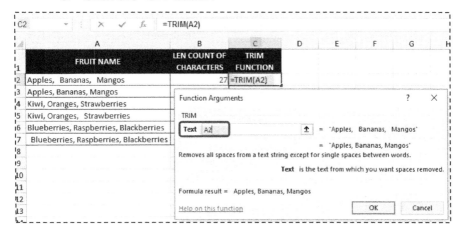

7. Copy the **TRIM** formula down cells '**C3**' thru '**C7**'
8. The extra spaces have been removed

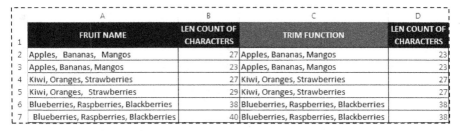

*Next we'll copy and **paste as values** the contents of column C and remove the columns (B & C) used for troubleshooting.*

9. Select cells '**C2**' thru '**C7**'
10. Click the '**Copy**' button or press **CTRL+C** from your keyboard
11. Select cell '**A2**'
12. **Right-click** and select '**Paste Special…**'
13. Select the '**Values**' radio button
14. Click the '**OK**' button

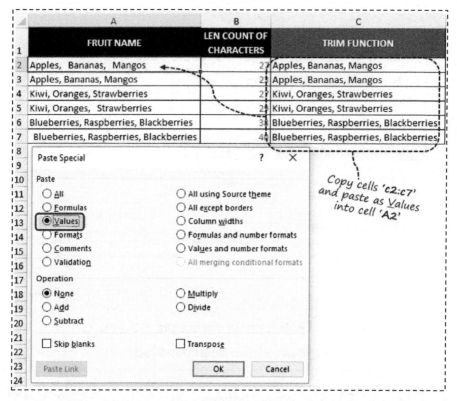

15. Select columns **'B'** & **'C'**

16. **Right-click** and select **'Delete'**, the troubleshooting columns **'B'** & **'C'** should now be removed

We have successfully removed all extraneous spaces from the records contained in **column 'A'**. Further analysis and reporting can be completed without error.

CHAPTER 15

Troubleshooting: How To Resolve Common Pivot Table Errors

Below are the two most common Pivot Table error messages with instructions on how to resolve them.

Please Note: The following is not a comprehensive list of all Pivot Table error messages, just a few of the more common ones.

Error message:

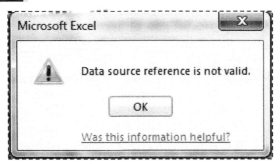

'Data source reference is not valid.'

Typically appears when you attempt to create a Pivot Table, with a **blank header row**.

To resolve, delete the blank row (in this case row 1) or make sure you select the correct header rows and supporting data before clicking **Insert : Pivot Table** from the Ribbon.

135

Error message:

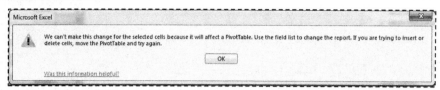

'We can't make this change for the selected cells because it will affect a PivotTable. Use the field list to change the report. If you are trying to insert or delete cells, move the PivotTable and try again.'

This message will appear when you attempt to change the column order, by cutting & pasting. For example, you want to move the '**Total**' column to be last the last.

Attempting to move a Column by Cutting & Pasting

	A	B	C	D	E
1					
2					
3	Row Labels	Sum of TOTAL	Sum of APPLES	Sum of ORANGES	Sum of MANGOS
4	Central	€ 138,571	€ 43,481	€ 53,278	€ 41,812
5	East	€ 145,588	€ 50,626	€ 47,117	€ 47,845
6	West	€ 196,787	€ 69,750	€ 65,259	€ 61,778
7	Grand Total	€ 480,946	€ 163,857	€ 165,655	€ 151,435

To change the column order in a Pivot Table, change the order in the PivotTables Fields pane:

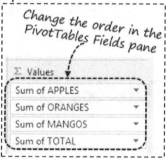

Change the order in the PivotTables Fields pane

Row Labels	Sum of APPLES	Sum of ORANGES	Sum of MANGOS	Sum of TOTAL
Central	€ 43,481	€ 53,278	€ 41,812	€ 138,571
East	€ 50,626	€ 47,117	€ 47,845	€ 145,588
West	€ 69,750	€ 65,259	€ 61,778	€ 196,787
Grand Total	€ 163,857	€ 165,655	€ 151,435	€ 480,946

This message will also appear when you attempt to delete a calculated field, row, or column. For example, you no longer want to see the row **'Grand Total'**, unfortunately, you can't simply delete this row, you'll receive the above error message.

19	100	$	10,339	$	2,585	16
20	Grand Total	$	480,946	$	7,515	

To remove **'Grand Total'** rows and columns we need to change the Pivot Table design.

1. Click the cell you would like to remove and then from the toolbar select **PIVOTTABLE TOOLS** and the tab **DESIGN**

2. Click the drop-down box for **'Grand Totals'** and select your preferred option:
    a. O<u>f</u>f for Rows and Columns
    b. O<u>n</u> for Rows and Columns
    c. On for <u>R</u>ows Only
    d. On for <u>C</u>olumns Only

For this example, we will select **'O<u>f</u>f for Rows and Columns'**

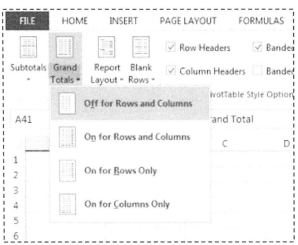

The **'Grand Total'** row has now been removed.

19	100	$	10,339	$	2,585	16
20						

A Message From The Author

Thank you!

Thank you for purchasing and reading this book, I hope you found it helpful! Your feedback is valued and appreciated! Please take a few minutes and leave a review.

Other Books Available From This Author

1. Microsoft® Excel® **Start Here** The Beginners Guide

2. The Step-By-Step Guide To The **25 Most Common** Microsoft® Excel® Formulas & Features

3. The Step-By-Step Guide To **Pivot Tables & ** Introduction To **Dashboards** *(version 2013)*

4. The Step-By-Step Guide To The **VLOOKUP** formula in Microsoft® Excel®

5. The Microsoft® Excel® Step-By-Step Training Guide **Book Bundle**

6. Excel® Macros & VBA For Business Users - A Beginners Guide

7. Microsoft® Word® Mail Merge The Step-By-Step Guide

Made in the USA
Middletown, DE
23 December 2018